THE GIFTS OF THE HOLY SPIRIT

THE GIFTS OF THE HOLY SPIRIT

CARLO MARIA MARTINI

Where the Spirit Burns

Course of Spiritual Exercises given by the
Cardinal to the Archdiocese of Milan

&

DOM PROSPER GUÉRANGER

The Gifts of the Holy Spirit

ST PAULS

Original Titles:

Copyright © 1997 I.T.L. S.p.A. – Via Antonio da Recanate 1
– 20124 Milano – Italia – *Dove Arde Lo Spirito*

Copyright © 1998 S.A. LA FROIDFONTAINE, 72300 Solesmes,
France – pour l'original français – *Le Dons du Saint-Esprit*

Translated by Andrew Tulloch

ST PAULS
Morpeth Terrace, London SW1P 1EP, United Kingdom
Moyglare Road, Maynooth, Co. Kildare, Ireland

English Language Copyright © ST PAULS (UK) 1998

ISBN 085439 546 6

Set by TuKan, High Wycombe
Produced in the EC
Printed by The Guernsey Press Co. Ltd., Guernsey, C.I.

ST PAULS is an activity of the priests and brothers of the
Society of St Paul who proclaim the Gospel through the media
of social communication

Contents

Introduction

The book you have in your hands presents two works by authors of note combined in a single volume. Both the deservedly influential Cardinal of Milan and the great Benedictine Liturgist of the last century explore the workings of the Holy Spirit in our lives, through the traditionally enumerated seven gifts.

Tradition has long distinguished these seven gifts, taking inspiration from Isaiah 11:1-2. This passage, as Martini notes, is a Messianic poem which describes the characteristics of the future Messiah (the Hebrew version of the Bible identifies six to which the Greek and Latin versions added a seventh). Christianity has of course identified this Messiah as Jesus of Nazareth, and it is Jesus who has the fullness of these characteristics or 'gifts'. But we who are baptised, and have been given the Spirit that was in him, have received these gifts too, by virtue of our baptism.

In the first book, the Cardinal of Milan, Carlo Maria Martini, shows how the gifts are actually present and active in the life of every Christian – and where we so often fail to take advantage of the very real strength and consolation they offer. In his own distinctive style, he draws on the Scriptures, his own experience and his wide contact with the experience of others through his pastoral ministry.

The contents of this first book originally took the form of *Spiritual Exercises* preached to the Diocese of Milan. However, as readers soon discover, they are included in a larger audience for whom these Exercises are relevant. Furthermore, the solid basis of these Exercises in the Scriptures and living experience is obvious from the outset. It could be argued that the rediscovery of these two elements – the value of the Scriptures and of ordinary Christians' personal and communal experience – constitutes the greatest strength of the present-day Church and a sign of hope. To read this book is to be invited to open yourself to the workings of the seven gifts and the action of the Spirit. In this process, the confidence and sureness that Martini displays is a great help to the reader on their own spiritual journey to God.

This book demonstrates that Martini not only knows how to express himself in a way that meets the ordinary present-day believer where they are: he also understands the dilemmas they face. But even more than that, he has seen that God is present to this believer and he has seen the hope that lies at the heart of our believing.

Some people are concerned that the Church is facing a crisis of huge dimensions. Martini diagnoses that our main problem lies in the fact that, personally and as a community of faith, we are not taking advantage of the gifts that God lavishes on us.

The great value of this book is twofold. It provides a challenge to believers today. At the same time it gives a deeply encouraging perspective on how the seven gifts are active in ordinary lives.

The second book, by Dom Prosper Guéranger, has already achieved something of classic status.

Guéranger (1805-75) was the first abbot of the reforming Benedictine Abbey of Solesmes in France. He is best known for his celebrated work, *The Liturgical Year* (last French edition in 5 vols 1948-51). This brief work, *The Gifts of the Holy Spirit,* has been published many times in various languages but is here made available for the first time in English.

As noted in the Foreword, the work was written well over 100 years ago and uses language and ideas that are not always easy for a modern reader. Guéranger belonged to a time when Catholicism, and Christianity in general, often expressed itself in a more severe and authoritative way than it necessarily does today. Then, the Church was less open to an understanding of the ambiguities involved in human experience than we are now, thanks, for instance, to the insights gained through psychology. Furthermore, while Martini takes as his foundation Scripture and experience, Guéranger explains the gifts from a more doctrinal point of view.

Nevertheless, the reader who perseveres will discover in Guéranger a genuine witness to the riches of the Catholic spiritual tradition. If they bear in mind the very real differences between the Catholic mentality of Guéranger's time and that of ours, the reader will find their understanding of the way the Spirit operates in our lives greatly enriched.

These two works present two complementary perspectives on the action of the Holy Spirit through the seven gifts. The two perspectives will enable the strength of the Catholic spiritual tradition, contemporary and 'traditional', to be discovered by those who did not know of it, and rediscovered and experienced by those who had forgotten it. They will see the value of the seven gifts and their basis in Scripture and everyday living.

Book I

Where the Spirit Burns

CARLO MARIA MARTINI

Foreword

The contents of this book were originally preached as *Spiritual Exercises* to a congregation gathered for four consecutive evenings in the Cathedral in Milan. In addition they were broadcast by radio and television to the people of the entire Diocese. Though the language inevitably reflects this origin, it is nonetheless extremely readable when transferred onto the written page.

Occasionally, as noted at various points in the text, the Cardinal makes a point about a word which makes sense in Italian, but obviously needs to be explained in an English translation.

1.

Gift of the Spirit is Piety

Reasons for and aims of the
Spiritual Exercises

Every time I begin a course of Spiritual Exercises I am always deeply moved, because one is dealing with a dramatic adventure of the Spirit. This evening the excitement and emotion is increased by the fact that, while we find ourselves in the splendid and historical basilica of St Ambrose, a few steps away from his tomb and at a distance of 1600 years from his death, we are joined – through radio or television – by tens of thousands of people of the Diocese, who in their homes or parishes, in deep communion with us, participate in our prayer during the Exercises.

This extraordinary initiative has been prompted by two anniversaries: firstly, there is the *Year of Saint Ambrose* (celebrated by us in the Diocese from 6 December 1996 and which we will conclude on 6 December 1997). Secondly and more importantly, we have the request of the Pope to dedicate this second year of preparation for the Millennium "to the sanctifying presence of the Spirit amongst the community of the disciples of Christ" (*Tertio Millennio Adveniente* No. 44).

To this end the local Church of Rome and other Churches in Italy have undertaken Diocesan and City missions; the Church of Bologna has hosted the (Italian) National Eucharist Congress. For our part, taking into consideration the large area occupied by the Diocese, together with the possibility of reaching all the parishes through the Diocesan radio and the television, we decided to opt for a form of event which is open to all – Spiritual Exercises. Even though they are being held in a reduced form – with only a single meditation each evening – these Exercises are designed to be a stimulus towards a true spiritual journey. John Paul II, in his *Apostolic Letter* "Operosam Diem", addressed to our Church of Milan on the occasion of the XVI centenary of the death of Ambrose, exhorted us to follow the instructions on the living of the Christian life given by our patron saint and spiritual guide, so that we can move more quickly and surely towards the prime objective of the Jubilee of the year 2000, that is, towards the reinvigoration of faith, hope, and witness.

This, therefore, is the purpose of the Exercises that we are about to begin.

However, against the background of a primary aim such as this, I want to suggest to each of you a question: In participating in the Exercises, what in particular do I propose to myself? What would I like to obtain in my spiritual life? What do I ask of the Lord?

For someone it might be the fruit of a good confession, or of the overcoming of a difficult moment; for another it might be an attainment of peace of heart or a reconciliation in the family, or perhaps a new step forward in prayer, or a more ardent faithfulness to Sunday Mass.

In short, whatever the intention the Holy Spirit makes us intuit, this will be the fruit and the grace of these days. Let us decide from the outset that these Exercises are to be truly *practical exercises* of the Spirit, in which one puts oneself on a path towards a precise end, with the help of the Lord invoked in prayer.

The theme of the Exercises

We will be meditating on the Holy Spirit and his gifts, a theme to which my recent Pastoral Letter *Three Tales of the Spirit* was dedicated, because the teaching on the gifts is of great use in order for us to become aware of the tremendous riches that come to us by baptism and by confirmation. A meditation on the Spirit and his gifts is of great use to stimulate us to bring to fruit such richness that we might conduct a more happy and more beautiful life, for ourselves and for others.

I would like to take as my point of departure – since it is the basis of the meditation on the gifts – a reflection that is fundamental to the theme of the entire Spiritual Exercises, a sort of little *anthropology of the Spirit*. To be precise, this 'anthropology' is a reminder of, and a recall to, that image of man and woman which the power of the Spirit of the Risen Jesus forms in us. And, immediately after, I will examine briefly as the first gift, that of 'piety'.

Let us place our journey then under the protection of Ambrose so that he, who was an illustrious master of the Spirit in the Latin Church, might be also interior master of each one of us. And let us put ourselves also under the protection of St Thérèse of the

Child Jesus, the first centenary of whose death we are celebrating and whose relics we venerated with joy a few days ago. May she, who was so docile to the gifts of the Spirit, help us with her intercession to penetrate into the riches – greater than all the treasures of the earth – that the Spirit instils in our hearts.

I – FUNDAMENTAL MEDITATION

1. The first introductory reflection will serve, as I was saying, to put the following reflections into context, and in this reflection I would like to comment on some words from the prophet Isaiah:

> A shoot shall come out from the stump of Jesse, and a branch shall grow out of his roots. The spirit of the Lord shall rest on him, the spirit of wisdom and understanding, the spirit of counsel and might, the spirit of knowledge and the fear of the Lord (Is 11:1-2).

These two verses begin a messianic poem in which the prophet describes the Messiah, a future descendant of David, Son of Jesse. The future descendant is compared to a branch, a twig that springs from the stump of a tree which had been blow over by a storm. There had been a storm, a hurricane, an earthquake and afterwards it seemed that all was dead: but instead a shoot grows, something new.

The shoot has certain characteristics, expressed in three pairs of nouns: wisdom-understanding, counsel-might (fortitude), knowledge-fear of the Lord.

To these six gifts – that we read of in the Hebrew Bible – the Greek and Latin Bibles have added the gift of piety. All seven of these characteristics, however, are those of a good king: a king wise in peace (as Solomon was wise, full of wisdom and understanding); a king astute and mighty in war (as David was full of counsel and might); a king pious and religious (as were Josiah and Hezekiah), and therefore full of knowledge and fear of the Lord.

One is speaking, then, of a great King, mysterious and future.

2. Who then is this King, who is so well endowed? In the first place the King is Jesus, on whom the New Testament asserts the Holy Spirit rests.

To speak of the Holy Spirit is to speak of a man, that is of Jesus. It was on him that the Spirit descended in fullness, and remains, dwells and rests. With Jesus the Spirit is at ease, as in his own home. The Spirit expressed himself best in the life of Jesus, Son of the Father. It is Jesus who has the fullness of the seven gifts.

Nevertheless, the passage from Isaiah alludes also to whoever lives in Jesus, is in Jesus. Primarily therefore, we think of Mary – "the Holy Spirit will descend upon you" (Lk 1:35) – who is the "Full of Grace". Then we think of every baptised person, each one of us who, in baptism, received these characteristics, these qualities.

Here begins the anthropology of the gifts of the Holy Spirit. St Ambrose first outlined such an anthropology, and it was developed in successive centuries reaching its height, we could say, in the thought of St Thomas Aquinas. Thomas, in fact, explains fully that, in order to be a Christian, it is necessary to have that 'totality' which we call faith, hope, charity. These theological virtues, however, are not sufficient in order to act in a godly way amongst the contradictions of the world and of history. It is necessary therefore that the Christian be docile to those movements of the Spirit that act along the lines of wisdom, understanding, counsel, fortitude, knowledge, piety, fear of God.

This Christian anthropology of the gifts is truly consoling: every Christian lives by faith, hope and charity. Faith is perfected by the spirit of understanding, knowledge and counsel; hope by the spirit of fear of God and by fortitude; charity expresses itself fully when it is perfected by piety and wisdom.

The Christian therefore is rich in virtues and gifts, and to the seven gifts correspond the Beatitudes:

> Blessed are the poor in spirit, for theirs is the kingdom of heaven. Blessed are those who mourn, for they will be comforted. Blessed are the meek, for they will inherit the earth. Blessed are those who hunger and thirst for righteousness, for they will be filled. Blessed are the merciful, for they will receive mercy. Blessed are the pure in heart, for they will see God. Blessed are the peacemakers, for they will be called children of God (Mt 5:3-9).

To these gifts moreover correspond that fruit of the Spirit which is mentioned by the apostle Paul: "The fruit of the Spirit is love, joy, peace, patience, kindness, generosity, faithfulness" (Gal 5:22).

All these together − virtues, gifts, Beatitudes, fruit of the Spirit − are a way of speaking about the exceptional richness and the immense vivacity of the life of grace. As Christians we have this life of grace and we must become aware of it; the Spirit fills us with gifts in order to draw us to the fullness found in the arms of God, to the eternal fullness.

Often we Christians are timid, timorous, we are not sufficiently daring, because in fact we are not aware of these gifts. When however – thanks perhaps to these Exercises that we are doing – we become conscious of them, the Christian life can flow in us like a stream, a torrent, a river.

How wonderful it would be if, also through the exhortation of my Pastoral Letter *Three Tales of the Spirit*, our Diocesan community were to discover the gifts present in her and if every Christian might be able to exclaim: What wonders the Holy Spirit has done in me!

II – THE GIFT OF PIETY

1. Let us now look, even if briefly, at the gift of piety, because it is this gift that will permit us to live these days of our Exercises well.

It is this gift in fact that gives us a taste for prayer and makes us pray willingly and with enthusiasm; it makes a prayer come from our heart that is fluid, serene and calm.

Often our prayer is forced, rigid, distracted, and it is precisely the gift of piety that makes us able to experience that prayer of the children who cry to God, calling him by the name of "Father!".

It is an exalted and extraordinary gift, a gift which accompanied all the earthly existence of Jesus. The following passage from the Gospel of Luke is in this regard very illuminating:

Now when all the people were baptised, and when Jesus also had been baptised and was praying, the heaven was opened, and the Holy Spirit descended upon him in bodily form like a dove. And a voice came from heaven, "You are my Son, the Beloved; with you I am well pleased" (Lk 3:21–22).

We notice first of all that the evangelist Luke, in his portrayal of the first public appearance of Jesus, has him in prayer. He appears as a *pray-er*, as one who prays. And he prays as Son, as was witnessed to by the voice from heaven, the voice of the Father: "You are my beloved Son".

Jesus lives the gift of piety profoundly because he feels the intimate delight of being Son, of calling God "Father". Already, at 12 years of age, he had said to Mary and Joseph when they found him in the temple: "Why were you searching for me? Did you not know that I must be in my Father's house?" (2:49).

The gift of piety therefore is the capacity

to speak with God as a child, tenderly; to praise him and adore him.

I wrote the following in the Pastoral Letter to which I have already referred: Piety is the disposition of the heart and of the entire life to adore God as Father and to offer him the worship that recognises him as the source and end of every authentic gift. Piety is tenderness for God, the being in love with him and desiring to give glory to him in everything. The mercy of the Lord towards us is so great that he desires to receive our charity! Thanks to piety, the Christian does not only search for the consolation that God brings, but desires to bear him company in his joy and in his sorrow for the sin of the world.

2. This gift finds expression in the lives of the Saints. The example of St Thérèse of the Child Jesus comes to mind: her spontaneity, for instance, in addressing herself to her heavenly Father, or the affection that filled her in her relationship with God. One day her sister Céline was struck by the sight of Thérèse who, while eagerly cooking seemed to be immersed in contemplation, and asked her: "'What are you thinking about?'. 'I am meditating on the Our Father', she responded, 'it is so sweet to call God our Father'. And the tears shone in her eyes" (*Counsels and Reminiscences*).

And the Saint herself, in the *Autobiographical Manuscript B*, confides: "It pleases Jesus to show me the way that leads to the divine furnace, that is the self-abandonment of a child who sleeps without fear in the arms of its Father".

Again, in a poetic composition of 7 June 1896, at a time when she had already felt the first attacks of her fatal illness and had already entered into the most extreme suffering of the spirit, she wrote: "My heaven lies in the always resting before my God, in the calling him 'Father'" (*Poems*).

The gift of piety, even if we are not conscious of it, because it is so profound, makes us look to God with childlike simplicity and truth.

3. The gift reveals itself also in the way one behaves with other people. It is the gift of sensitivity in human relations, and it allows us to deal with all lovingly and with great understanding. On this point Pope Paul VI, whom I had the good fortune to know well, comes to mind: deeply respectful towards all and thoughtful with all. If, in fact, we have the spirit of piety, which places us before God as Father, it comes naturally to us to see everyone as a child of God and loved by him. It is therefore a gift that by its very nature permeates daily life, family life, the relations

of every day, rendering them attractive, easy and enjoyable. It is a gift that removes the thorns, shields us from the blows, and smooths the rough corners of our relationships.

4. It is interesting to observe that the spiritual tradition, when asking itself what is the attitude contrary to piety, did not name impiety – impiety means the despising of God and all that is sacred – but hardness of heart, insensitivity and the inability to understand other people. Hardness of heart is the effect of not feeling oneself to be a child of God, of not believing him to be a good Father; and so, as a consequence, one treats both God and one's brothers and sisters badly.

I would like to underline the social importance of the gift of piety. Starting with a prayer that is affectionate and filial, this gift permeates everywhere with its beneficial effects: in the relationships of children with parents, of parents with children, of spouses amongst themselves; in the relations at work, of friendship, in the parish, community, group, because its very substance is that of an attentiveness, a respect and a sensitivity.

A brief examination of conscience

I think that it would be useful to conclude with a few questions for a brief examination of conscience.

1. *How do I recite the Our Father* that St Thérèse of the Child Jesus recited almost in tears at the thought of having God for a Father?

2. *How do I overcome the anxieties of life and its moments of anguish?* Do I know how to throw myself with faith into the arms of God, knowing that he is my Father and for this reason nothing in the world can do me any lasting harm?

The gift of piety extinguishes this anguish, it conquers and overcomes.

3. *Do I treat with a loving respect other people* of my own house, neighbours, and those with whom I find myself every day?

Piety is a virtue that is exercised first of all in the family, with thoughtful attention towards whoever is close to us. Perhaps here we can let go of the excuse of being concerned about those far away or with those whom we will never meet – because obviously it is easier to deal with people we do not see! But piety is the gift of short and simple relations with God – a spontaneous, immediate and trusting prayer – and with other people.

2.
Gift of the Spirit is Wisdom

The gift of wisdom comes first in the list of the seven gifts. Its use in the language of our own time is similar to that of the word 'piety'. The word piety – on which we reflected in the preceding meditation and which indicates the exalted gift of a filial love of God – as it is used ordinarily today, refers to something not entirely noble or even authentic. Likewise, the word 'wisdom' is today out of fashion. It seems to allude to something mysterious (the wisdom of the ancients), and is substituted by the word 'knowledge'.* This is particularly true of *scientific* knowledge, and often it is the

---

* The Italian word used here is *scienza* and therefore could also be translated into English as 'science', hence the Cardinal's point about the total identifiction of knowledge with *scientific* knowledge that is often made.

scientist who counts and not the wise or learned person.

And yet the noun 'wisdom' and the objectives 'learned' and 'wise' are amongst the most common terms in the Bible. An entire biblical book is entitled *Wisdom* or the *Wisdom of Solomon*, and forms part of a series of books known as the *Wisdom* books (Job, Proverbs, Ecclesiastes and Ecclesiasticus).

What does it mean then, the word 'wisdom' that the Scriptures hold to be so important?

I would like to structure my response to such a question in five steps, a bit like the five steps that ascend to the altar of this Basilica of St Ambrose. These steps are: the wisdom of Jesus; the wisdom of the Christian; the wisdom of the Cross; the gift of wisdom; the opposite of wisdom, that is mediocrity, foolishness and stupidity.

I – THE WISDOM OF JESUS

1. The wisdom of Jesus appears in the Gospel according to Matthew from the moment of the inaugural discourse at Nazareth:

When he came to Nazareth, where he had been brought up, he went to the synagogue on the Sabbath day, as was his

30

custom. He stood up to read, and the scroll of the prophet Isaiah was given to him. He unrolled the scroll and found the place where it was written: "The Spirit of the Lord is upon me, because he has anointed me to bring good news to the poor. He has sent me to proclaim release to the captives and recovery of sight to the blind, to let the oppressed go free, to proclaim the year of the Lord's favour." And he rolled up the scroll, gave it back to the attendant, and sat down. The eyes of all in the synagogue were fixed on him. Then he began to say to them, "Today this scripture has been fulfilled in your hearing" (Lk 4:16–21).

In order to understand properly the sense of this passage from Luke, we might place beside it the parallel found in Mark which, in describing the discourse of Jesus, underlines that the people were astonished when they heard him and exclaimed: "Where did this man get all this? What is this wisdom that has been given to him?" (Mk 6:2).

We might ask ourselves at this point how exactly this discourse of Jesus is one of wisdom or why Jesus shows himself wise in explaining the Scriptures.

Let us look again at some of the elements in this passage, beginning at the moment in which the passage becomes most intense and full of meaning.

• Jesus speaks at *Nazareth*, where he had learnt the human wisdom which however was not sufficient to enable him to pronounce these words. For this reason the words must have come from God, not from the education that he had received.

• He speaks on the *Sabbath*, on the sacred day; he speaks in the *synagogue*, in a sacred place.

• He reads a prophetic passage from the *Scriptures*, which constitute the *Holy Book par excellence*. The passage concerns the future Messiah, and Jesus declares, "Today these Scriptures have been fulfilled in your hearing".

Jesus shows himself to be wise because by his word he *opens the mystery of history*, hidden for centuries in the pages of the prophets: he affirms that the mystery is there present, that it is he himself who makes it present, who makes the kingdom present, who reveals the plan of God. He fulfils therefore an outstanding act of wisdom, revealing the mystery of the Kingdom, and is wise because he is intimate with the mysteries of God and these mysteries are 'connatural' to him (i.e. are part of his very nature).

The *wisdom of Jesus*, seen in the light of this passage from Luke, consists in his knowledge born of experience – through 'connaturality' – of the mystery of the Kingdom, to the point where he is able to affirm: *it is here, I am it.* It is his knowledge born of experience of the salvific will of God that allows him to proclaim this will. It is the knowledge of the mystery of God rooted in the Trinity, of which he is a part and whose reality he expresses.

In other words, the wisdom of Jesus is his capacity to embrace the entire mystery of God as one who stands inside it and who sees it in all its dimensions; it is his capacity to embrace the entire mystery of history as one who is at the origins of this history and is at the same time above it.

Jesus is wise in the highest degree because in him all is fulfilled, all reaches perfection and in him all is revealed.

2. There is another important text that proclaims the centrality of Jesus in the mystery of God, this time not from the gospels but from a letter of St Paul:

Paul, an apostle of Christ Jesus by the will of God, to the saints who are in Ephesus and are faithful in Christ Jesus: Grace to you and peace from God our Father and the Lord Jesus Christ. Blessed be the God and Father of our Lord Jesus Christ, who has blessed us in Christ with every spiritual blessing in the heavenly places, just as he chose us in Christ before the foundation of the world to be holy and blameless before him in love. He destined us for adoption as his children through Jesus Christ, according to the good pleasure of his will, to the praise of his glorious grace that he freely bestowed on us in the Beloved. In him we have redemption through his blood, the forgiveness of our trespasses, according to the riches of his grace that he lavished on us. With all wisdom and insight he has made known to us the mystery of his will, according to his good pleasure that he set forth in Christ, as a plan for the fullness of time, to gather up all things in him, things in heaven and things on earth (Eph 1:1-10).

Let us note how the affirmation of the centrality of Christ is repeated: in him, in Christ, in the Son. We are told that: "(God) has blessed us in Christ"; that "he chose us in Christ"; that "his glorious grace" was "freely bestowed on us in the Beloved"; that "in him (Christ) we have redemption through his blood"; and that God's plan "for the fullness of time" is to "gather up all things in him (Christ); things in heaven and things on earth". The Apostle, with this wonderful hymn, teaches us that Christ, being at the centre of the divine plan, comprehends it and embraces all of it. Jesus is the very wisdom of God, which knows and penetrates every mystery of God and of Man. Because of this St Paul, at the end of the hymn, prays in the desire that "the Father of glory" might give to all Christians "a spirit of wisdom and revelation as you come to know him (fully)" (cf v.17).

II – THE WISDOM OF THE CHRISTIAN

From the wisdom of Jesus, which knows and understands all, is born the wisdom of the Christian as a participation in that of Jesus. This wisdom is the gift to see things as Jesus sees them, to see things as the Lord discerns them from on high; it is the gift to see the relation of all things to the mystery of the Trinity.

The creature who more than any other was possessed of such a gift is Mary. She was wise in the highest way permissible to humanity. If we recite slowly the Canticle of the Magnificat, we realise that Mary contemplated all happenings from the point of view of God, who "has scattered the proud in the thoughts of their hearts... and lifted up the lowly... has filled the hungry with good things, and sent the rich away empty" (cf Lk 1:46-55). Hers was the contemplation of history from the perspective of God and from the perspective of the poor. This is not a contemplation of history as it is seen by human beings, that is from the perspective of the victors.

As the wisdom of Mary is the participation in the wisdom of Jesus, so is the wisdom of the Christian.

III – THE WISDOM OF THE CROSS

The third step is the wisdom of the Cross. The wisdom of God which is given to the Christian to participate in is, in fact, the wisdom of the Cross. It distinguishes clearly the wisdom of God and of the Christian from all the wisdoms of this world, which are founded on efficiency, on results, on success, on money and on power. Contemplating the Cross of Christ, the Christian discovers that, contrary to the path marked out by these other wisdoms, the Kingdom of God passes through humility, insignificance, adversities, and also through the Cross and death.

To discover this is truly a great gift. Without the gift of the Holy Spirit, it is not possible to exercise the wisdom of the Cross, because it is repugnant to the normal way of seeing things, that looks for only that which is 'worthwhile' and that which succeeds. To

grasp the mystery of God amongst contradictions, poverty and in the face of Jesus
crucified means that one has the wisdom of
the Christian. Therefore, to understand the
Cross is to understand life and to understand
human existence and ourselves.

IV – THE GIFT OF WISDOM

What then is the gift of wisdom, which is
given to each of us with baptism, and which
the Spirit continually makes present, moving
us interiorly?

Wisdom is the gift that enables us to see
all with the eyes of God, with his gaze, and to
see all from 'on high'. It is the gift to see
events and situations as they are seen by Jesus
crucified and resurrected, from the height of
the Cross and the glory of the Resurrection.
To be able to see them from the 'on high' and
from the centre. It enables us to see things
not from the perspective given us by a single
piece of information or intellectual light but
rather by divine instinct, by connaturality,
(which is, as we said before, by something
being natural to us). St Thomas Aquinas,
speaking of the gifts of the Spirit, uses often
the expression: as by divine instinct.

We see as by divine instinct because we are
in Jesus who is at the centre, and we are in
God who is above all.

The *understanding by connaturality* for this reason can be compared to taste and is called 'wisdom' – which means precisely flavour, something with flavour or taste. We experience it as soon as we notice that a decision, a taking of position or a choice *is or is not according to the Kingdom of God*. But we notice it through supernatural instinct. Just as I know that a food is sweet or savoury not by reasoning, nor by chemical analysis of the components of the salt or sugar, but rather by the reaction of my taste buds, so similarly, the Christian moved by the Spirit realises that something is or is not according to the plan of God, that it is alright or not alright, that it is in conformity or is not in conformity with the Gospel. And they notice it more by way of the heart than by way of the mind: therefore this gift is linked to charity, to love more than to intelligence. It is the intelligence of love and of the heart.

We could say, in brief, that wisdom is *a delectable and loving penetration of the mysteries of God:* of the mystery of the Trinity, of the mystery of the Cross, of the mysteries of the Kingdom and of the mystery of history.

Such wisdom is also given to the most simple of people, in fact more to them than to others. Jesus says: "I thank you, Father, Lord of heaven and earth, because you have hidden these things from the wise and the

intelligent and have revealed them to infants"
(Mt 11:25).

In connection with this thought there
comes to mind a most beautiful page from
the blessed Contardo Ferrini, a gifted and
cultured man, a university professor at Pavia,
a City Councillor of Milan, who greatly
loved the mountains:

> Many times, tired after a longer day walk-
> ing in the mountains, seated in the shade
> of a fir tree that shielded me from the
> rays of the setting sun, I have had con-
> versations with a shepherd of the Alps or
> with a poor woman, a daughter of the
> mountains! And every time I was amazed
> and confused: such a sense of divine Provi-
> dence, such a low estimation of earthly
> things, such an intimate peace and joy of
> a life lived without fear! (C. Ferrini,
> *Religious Writings*).

Thus the gift of wisdom is in simple people.
For my own part, when I have visited the
sick and elderly and talked with them and
listened to them, I have often exclaimed:
"What wisdom, the gift of God!" "What
upright judgement!" "What capacity to understand the value of certain things and the
relative worthlessness of others!"

I do not mean to say that wisdom is found

only among the more simple and humble. It is surely a gift that touches everybody's life in all its aspects, even the most mundane. However, as the gift of piety expresses itself best in filial prayer and especially in the great liturgical prayers, so it seems to me that the gift of wisdom expresses itself best in a privileged way, in 'public' wisdom, in the governing of public things and in politics. To engage in politics also calls for wisdom and not only competence or cunning. In this case wisdom is the gift that enables one to place individual problems in a larger picture, in the picture of the common good. It is a gift that is very necessary for those who have public responsibilities. We often complain about our politicians, but do we pray for them, asking for them the gift of wisdom?

The Bible calls that which is opposed to wisdom by diverse names – mediocrity, foolishness, stupidity – and speaks often about this attitude which is contrary to wisdom.

Essentially, foolishness is the *lack of taste for the things of God, a lack of a sense of God, of a sense of mystery and of a sense of Providence*. It is a lack that makes us blind and lost, and it is at the origin of many anxieties and fears, and much mental confusion.

I would like here to mention briefly three simple biblical examples of foolishness, of this lack of wisdom.

• In Luke 12:16ff Jesus tells the parable of a landowner who, after he had enlarged his granaries in order to gather all his grain and all his goods into them, decided to take his ease, to eat, drink and amuse himself. But God said to him, "Foolish man, this very night your life will be asked of you". This is the story of a man who made his plans without taking God, death or the shortness of life into account. His is the centuries-old mediocrity of one who lives with their head in the sand, occupying themselves only with the present.

• But there is a case of an even more pro-found mediocrity which is reproved in the New Testament. And it is Jesus who pro-nounces the reproach when addressing him-self to the two disciples at Emmaus: "Oh foolish and slow of heart to believe!" (Lk 24:25). This is the foolishness of one who does not perceive the design of God in ob-scure events or those which run contrary to common expectations; it is the foolishness of one who makes their plans without taking the Cross into account.

• We find the third example in Matthew 7:25, where Jesus is speaking of the foolishness of a man who built his house on sand and who did not know of the Gospel way of living expressed in the Sermon on the Mount. His is a foolish life, mediocre because he does not put into practice the teachings of Jesus. This mediocrity is that of this foolish disciple, that mediocrity which brings one to ruin.

These are examples of the mediocrity of the single individual, but it is also a mediocrity which can strike a parish community, a group, or a movement, as if they were founded on sand. These communal bodies are founded on sand when they do not recognise that Gospel way of life which is expressed in chapter 18 of Matthew's Gospel. In this chapter we discover that the way of life for a community and its members consists in making oneself small, in not demanding the first place, in respecting the weakest, in taking care of one's brother, in respecting authority, in loving the common prayer and in forgiving offences.

A community that does not found itself on these Gospel values does not have the wisdom of God.

In this meditation then, we have tried to understand what is the wisdom of Jesus, of Mary and of the Christian; what is the wisdom of the Cross; what is the gift of wisdom in contrast to foolishness and mediocrity.

Before considering a few points for reflection, let us first of all thank God who has placed us on this path, who desires to fill us with such a gift, and let us beg him to allow us to be filled by it.

I want to add here an important clarification: the gift of the Spirit is not something that we can necessarily feel or perceive. If this were my approach I might be able to think, reflect, complete a work of introspection and thus discover wisdom inside me. This is not the way it works. Instead, wisdom is an instinctive gift. I notice its presence after it has operated, saying, "But how the Lord helped me to judge well on that difficult occasion!"; or "That person truly had an apt word!" One realises what has happened, therefore, afterwards.

Anyone who pretends to have this gift, risks distorting and spoiling it. Anyone who on the other hand entrusts themselves to the Holy Spirit, invoking him with simplicity, will then realise – perhaps during an examination of conscience or a review of life – that the gift had in fact been present and operating. It is not necessary that we should feel it, because the Spirit has no need to make himself felt in order to act in us.

Three questions for a moment of silence

I would like to conclude by suggesting to you three questions for a moment of silence.

1. What place do *the designs of God* have in my life, in my programmes and projects? Do I

occasionally reflect more widely on the plan that God has for me, for my life and for history? Do I manage to have an encouraging vision for my life or do I allow myself to be confined by timid and restricted visions?

Wisdom, widening our hearts and our horizons, helps us to know, to perceive, almost to 'scent' the part which the plan of God has in our lives.

2. What place has the *wisdom of the Cross* in my life? Do I grasp its positive significance in negative events, or do these events disturb me, crush me, irritate me, making me angry with myself, with other people, with life and with everything? Do I cultivate the wisdom of the Cross or am I foolish and slow of heart to believe in the work of God in me, even through the Cross?

3. Do I nourish myself on the bread of wisdom, which is the *Scriptures*, and the Gospels in particular? Do I nourish myself on the bread of wisdom, which is the Eucharist, which gives us the sense of Christ, which introduces us into the heart of his mystery and therefore, by connaturality, makes us participate in this gift of wisdom?

Let us ask for the gift of wisdom for ourselves, for others, for the Church and for all of humanity.

3.
Gift of the Spirit is the Fear of God

Let us call upon the Holy Spirit so that he might give us the gift of the fear of God. Let us pray to that Spirit of whom St Ambrose wrote in his work *The Six Days of Creation*: "The Spirit is like a fire that incinerates all that is material and earthly, approves of all that is sincere and improves all that his flame touches".

We will consider in this third meditation 'the fear of God', distancing ourselves, so to speak, from the traditional biblical order that makes 'understanding' and 'counsel' follow-on from 'wisdom'.

This order in which we list the gifts is different for two reasons. The first reason concerns the structure of our discussion, because we are trying to link the gifts of the Spirit to the great theological virtues – charity, hope and faith. We began with piety and wisdom which perfect the virtue of charity; and now we are reflecting on the fear of God which is an aspect, a perfection, of hope. In the next chapter we will stop to look at the gifts of counsel and knowledge which are connected with faith.

Besides the structural reason there is a second reason which I will call 'dynamic', in reference to the 'journey' that we are making during these Exercises. Spiritual Exercises, in fact, are an itinerary composed of stages even if our own, being on a bit of a reduced scale, do not show these stages clearly. They begin with a call to prayer, with a recovery of the strengths found in prayer and of the gift of piety. Then we put ourselves before the divine plan for creation and redemption – the so-called beginning and boundation – and in order to grasp this plan the gift of wisdom is necessary. Standing before the plan of God, we understand the evil that is in us, our sin, and therefore the third stage is that of repentance and of fear. We are for this reason, in this third meditation, in a privileged moment for making a good sacramental confession. We are in a *penitential* moment, and it is therefore important to consider the fear of God.

And yet, we find ourselves once again before a word that is apparently slightly obsolete. The expression 'fear of God' or 'holy fear of God' is not used in modern-day language and in fact tends to disturb us: the Christian religion is a religion of love, and so why do we find fear numbered among the gifts of the Spirit? Perhaps this word evokes for us images of educational methods that are archaic, now superseded and founded on fear and intimidation! But how can one fear God who is love, mercy and goodness?

These are questions that we each carry inside of us.

And yet we know that the 'fear of God' and the attitude of 'fearing God' are, as we have seen in case of wisdom, some of the most frequently used expressions in the First Testament. The fear of God is strictly connected with wisdom: to fear God is the summation of the entire biblical religiosity, and it is a very noble human attitude. In this regard I cite a passage from the book of Ecclesiasticus:

> The fear of the Lord is glory and exultation, and gladness and a crown of rejoicing. The fear of the Lord delights the heart, and gives gladness and joy and long life. Those who fear the Lord will have a happy end; on the day of their death they will be blessed. To fear the Lord is the beginning of wisdom; she is created with the faithful in the womb. She made among human beings an eternal foundation, and

among their descendants she will abide faithfully. To fear the Lord is fullness of wisdom; she inebriates mortals with her fruits... The fear of the Lord is the crown of wisdom, making peace and perfect health to flourish... To fear the Lord is the root of wisdom, and her branches are long life (Ecclus 1:11-16,18,20).

Thus the fear of the Lord is not something that crushes, but which expands the heart, cheers us up, gives gladness and rejoicing; it is the beginning, fullness, crown and root of wisdom. It is not by chance that the Bible holds in honour the one who fears God. One is dealing with an extremely noble attitude, positive, very desirable and something to be encouraged today, we might say.

Let us seek to understand, then, what is meant by 'fear of God'. I would like to approach a deeper appreciation of this gift by way of three stages: Jesus lives the fear of God; Jesus commands respect and strikes fear; and the fear as a gift in the life of the Christian.

I – JESUS LIVES THE FEAR OF GOD

First of all I want to emphasise that the fear of God – in its true significance – was present in Jesus who lived with *profound reverence before the Father* and his will. Perhaps the greatest expression of such reverence is the prayer of Gethsemane: "Father, if you are willing, remove this cup from me; yet, not my will but yours be done" (Lk 22:42).

Each one of you, reading the Gospels, will easily be able to find the places in which this loving and reverential fear of Jesus before the Father is expressed.

II – JESUS INSTILS FEAR

I am concerned above all to dwell on another aspect in the life of Jesus, one which creates for us a greater difficulty: his hard words, cutting words, which instil fear, his threats.

Here I quote two passages from the evangelist Luke which contain a series of four 'woes', of threatening words, often forgotten by us, but which follow on from the Beatitudes.

> But woe to you who are rich, for you have received your consolation. Woe to you who are full now, for you will be hungry. Woe to you who are laughing now, for you will mourn and weep. Woe to you when all speak well of you, for that is what their ancestors did to the false prophets (Lk 6:24–26).

49

Woe to you, Chorazin! Woe to you, Bethsaida! For if the deeds of power done in you had been done in Tyre and Sidon, they would have repented long ago, sitting in sackcloth and ashes. But at the judgement it will be more tolerable for Tyre and Sidon than for you. And you, Capernaum, will you be exalted to heaven? No, you will be brought down to Hades (Lk 10:13-15).

The 'pedagogy' or teaching method of Jesus is truly a method of fear, and the curses pronounced against the two cities of Galilee make one think.

Another context in the Gospels where we find 'woes' are those pronounced against the scribes, the pharisees and the doctors of the Law. All are extremely grave admonitions which today still touch those who have, in the Church or in society, some sort of knowledge, power or responsibility.

Then the Lord said to him, "Now you Pharisees clean the outside of the cup and of the dish, but inside you are full of greed and wickedness. You fools!... Woe to you who neglect justice and the love of God... you who love to have the seat of honour in the synagogues... Woe to you who load people with burdens hard to bear, and you yourselves do not lift a finger to ease them (cf Lk 11:39–47).

Again, I remember the series of threats pronounced against Jerusalem, when Jesus wept over the Holy City:

> If you, even you, had only recognised on this day the things that make for peace! But now they are hidden from your eyes. Indeed, the days will come upon you, when your enemies will set up ramparts around you and surround you, and hem you in on every side. They will crush you to the ground, you and your children within you, and they will not leave within you one stone upon another; because you did not recognise the time of your visitation from God (Lk 19:42-44).

From all these passages and from other similar ones we realise that Jesus was not afraid to use strong language, nor to instil fear. We might ask ourselves why this is so – is there perhaps a pedagogy of fear present in the way Jesus acts?

It is not easy to respond to such a question, and I would like simply to take a closer look at least at the words which we first quoted, those following on from the Beatitudes:

But woe to you who are rich, for you have received your consolation. Woe to you who are full now, for you will be hungry. Woe to you who are laughing now, for you will mourn and weep. Woe to you when all speak well of you, for that is what their ancestors did to the false prophets (Lk 6:24–26).

An objection spontaneously arises: When all's said and done what wrong is there in having riches, in eating to satiety, in laughing or in enjoying a little fame? If we examine the words of Jesus attentively, we realise that they have nothing to do with a moralistic pedagogy. He does not say, woe to you who revel in luxury, woe to you thieves, woe to you murderers, woe to you who use violence. These would be obvious words. Jesus goes further than this in order to *educate his hearers to responsibility and to the realisation of the seriousness of the moment.* His is a pedagogy of responsibility: the Kingdom is here, with its supreme values, the Kingdom is Jesus, and woe then to whoever attaches themselves to mundane values as if they were the ultimate ones. Such a person will perish together with those values.

The pedagogy of Jesus is not, therefore, one of fear. Rather he teaches us that whoever places their trust in worldly values,

whoever refutes the primacy of the Kingdom, signs their own condemnation and digs
a ditch for themselves.

There is also a pedagogical function of
fear, which is to make one responsible and to
enable one to understand the seriousness of
the Gospel. In lay terms we would say that it
helps us to understand the sense of the seriousness of human existence and of responsibility for one's own actions; the sense of
responsibility towards other people, above all
towards the weakest; the sense of the responsibility for the earth and for the cosmos.

III – THE GIFT OF THE FEAR OF GOD

The pedagogy of Jesus is very important, but
it is still not yet the actual gift of the fear of
God, which supposes these things but goes
beyond them.

Certainly the gift of fear is linked to the
seriousness of life, to the urgency of the
Kingdom and to responsibility. Nevertheless,
it is something much more delicate, much
more profound, much more subtle, and is
something capable of opening the heart and
thawing the spirit.

The gift of the fear of God is a love of
God which is conscious of its own fragility,
therefore conscious also of the possibility to

offend God and to lose his friendship. It is an attitude of great reverence towards a mystery that overwhelms us on every side, that we do not possess, that we do not hold in our hands, because it is continually given to us as a gift and we continually have the possibility of rejecting it, losing it and neglecting it. The fear of God sees moral action not as a simple obedience to a law but rather as a relationship with a person; a personal relationship with God the Father and with the Lord Jesus. For this reason the fear of God allows us to live our moral actions with all the thoughtfulness, the respect, the diligence, and the affection that expresses a true relationship with a person and which calls for a relationship with God Himself, Father and Son.

The *gift of the fear of God is the knowledge that God is* – according to the well-known expression – a *mysterium fascinans*, a mystery that attracts and fascinates by its very lovability. Together with this is the knowledge that God is also a *mysterium tremendum*, with which one cannot toy, which questions us profoundly and seriously, precisely because it is a love which is total and all-demanding, a personal relationship of *covenant* and of *gift*.

The divine mystery cannot be trivialised.

In this sense, the fear of God is a sign of maturity, of a high morality, of a lived responsibility and of an authentic religiosity.

In practice, this gift is a combination of attitudes that enables us to overcome the banality, the superficiality, the haste with which, for example, we pray or enter into church or live the sacraments. It is a gift that purifies, and God later puts us to the test through darknesses and nights of the spirit, so that this gift of fear develops.

John of the Cross, Doctor of the Church and a great mystic, on the subject of the purification of the spirit, affirms that "In its relations with God the soul feels born in itself a greater gentleness and reverence, qualities that must always preside over its relations with God" (John of the Cross, *Dark Night of the Soul,* I, 12.3).

It seems to me here useful to give a contemporary example of the gift of the fear of God.

I received recently the diary of a young woman of our Diocese, who died from a serious tumour on the 13th of last May aged 26, having been married for two years. It is extraordinary to find in the pages written by Christina (that being the name of the young woman) the enormous will to be healed, to live, and to have children, coupled with the openness to the gift of the Holy Spirit to let herself be guided on the paths of love, of faith, of hope and of the fear of God.

It is truly an exceptional testimony to

the Holy Spirit, and I will here quote some words written a few days before her death:

> I am very calm and I feel the breath of God on me, which is trying to help me but is not able to do so as fully as it might because I am still not a pure soul, in which he can freely express his will. This I feel, even though I only desire to do what he wants, to receive what he has in store for me: only his will.

This is the gift of the fear of God: the fear of being lacking, of not being equal to so much Love, with at the same time the strong desire to be totally of God. She adds:

> I rejoice and I remain astonished, like a baby, at so much love, joy, mercy and charity, and I think that I am extremely fortunate to have love as a heavenly Father, and when the most infinitesimal splinter of him strikes me and pervades me, it is a sensation so strong that words will never succeed in describing it.

There would still be much to write on the gift of fear of God, linked with the other gifts. I should also have to speak about the attitudes which are contrary to the fear of

God, like superficiality, slovenliness, and a slapdash attitude in prayer and in life.

Time however does not allow this, and so I move on to put three questions to you.

Three questions for a moment of silence

1. *How do I begin prayer?* How do I begin *the important actions of life?* How do I go to the significant encounters of life? Perhaps I go any old how, rushing headlong into things almost as if I were forever trying to board a moving bus? Or perhaps before prayer I dedicate a moment to reflect and realise what I am about to do? Or also before speaking a word I think about it, before I begin an important encounter or task, I pause for a moment in order to recollect myself?

The fear of God is the learning of respect before the mystery of God, of things, and of people. Nothing must be trivialised, nothing must be completed in haste, superficially and distractedly. And we must not be surprised if, taking everything any old how, chalking up one action after another, prayer does not nourish us, the Eucharist and the sacraments do not edify us, and meetings with people tire us and weigh us down. A slovenly and badly conducted liturgy is a sign of a lack of the fear of God.

The first question therefore concerns the beginnings of our days.

2. *When I feel remorse, why do I feel it?* Perhaps I feel it because I have been inconsistent or because I have cut a ridiculous figure? Or is it rather because I have disappointed the expectations that God had of me? The type of remorse that I experience announces the kind of love that I live. The Spirit moves us from a servile and self-interested fear of lacking, to a humble and filial fear, which gives peace of heart, in the certainty of the forgiveness of the Father.

3. *What is my sense of responsibility towards other people, above all towards the weakest?* And what sense of responsibility do I have towards nature and the environment? All these things are made by God and are to be respected, and naturally to be venerated. This is especially true of the image of God in the poor, in the suffering, in the elderly, in the marginalised and in every person who is in difficulty. This was the great gift of Mother Teresa of Calcutta: the profound reverence towards the poor, the dying, and the diseased. It is a sign of the fear of God.

How can I express, therefore, not only my solidarity with others, as I might do in helping other people, but also my respect for anyone I may chance to meet, wherever and whenever?

In conclusion, the fear of God is by no means a thing of the past. It is the guarantee of a good life; it is the pledge of a just and fraternal society; it is the guardian of the future of a people and of humanity, and it is a sign of closeness to the mystery of God.

4.

Gifts of the Spirit are Counsel and Knowledge

We will begin this meditation immediately with a passage from the Gospel of Luke. In our meditations we have been focusing on certain episodes reported by Luke which express the gifts of the Holy Spirit in the life of Jesus. We contemplated in the first place the scene of the *Baptism of Jesus* in order to see in him the gift of piety (chapter 3 of Luke's Gospel). Then we recalled the *inaugural discourse of Jesus* at Nazareth in order to understand the gift of wisdom (chapter 4). In the last chapter we reflected on the threats pronounced by Jesus in various passages of Luke in order to consider the gift of the fear of God (chapters 6, 10, 11 and 19).

Now, our point of departure is taken once more from chapter 6 of Luke's Gospel, but this time in order to speak of *the gift of counsel* and afterwards, more briefly, of *the gift of knowledge.*

I – THE GIFT OF COUNSEL IN JESUS

On another Sabbath he entered the synagogue and taught, and there was a man there whose right hand was withered. The scribes and the Pharisees watched him to see whether he would cure on the Sabbath, so that they might find an accusation against him. Even though he knew what they were thinking, he said to the man who had the withered hand, "Come and stand here." He got up and stood there. Then Jesus said to them, "I ask you, is it lawful to do good or to do harm on the Sabbath, to save life or to destroy it?" After looking around at all of them, he said to him, "Stretch out your hand." He did so, and his hand was restored (Lk 6:6-10).

The central problem in this passage is not so much that of the healing, expressed in one line in the last verse, it is rather a problem of *discernment*, of a *conflict of interpretations.* On one hand there is a sick man in the synagogue, and Jesus has the power to heal him; on the other hand there is the law which forbids – according to a certain interpretation – one to do anything on the holy day of the Sabbath. It is a good thing to observe the law and it is also a good thing to meet a human need; the law is good and compassion for a sick person is good.

Conflicts between different duties have always been frequent, particularly in today's world. Here we touch on an important point of morality: morality does not consist simply in doing good and avoiding evil. If it were so, it would all be very easy. The problem is infinitely more complex, because it is necessary to ask oneself: *in this particular circumstance, what is truly good and what is truly evil?* And in particular, between two goods which clash with each other and which exclude each other, which must I choose? How should I act when faced with a lesser evil when it is precisely the only possible greater good? How can I discern which of two interpretations of a law is the more true? In general, how do we survive amidst the complexities of life, the tangling of opinions, the clashing of cultures and moralities and the contrast between religions?

These are all things that give rise to doubts, mental confusion, anxiety, impediments to action, bad consciences, and cowardice in the giving up of oneself to the opinion of the moment.

But Jesus overcomes this conflict in a surefooted and decisive manner, even though he knows that his choice in favour of the man who needs to be healed will cost him dearly and that he will have to pay the price. He exercises in conjunction the *spirit of counsel* and the *spirit of fortitude* of which we will speak in the next meditation.

We are invited to contemplate Jesus as he demonstrates his capacity to come out of this conflict of interpretations with decisiveness, and as he moves easily through the meanders of contrasting opinions and knows how to find with few words the reasons for the correct decision: "Is it lawful to do good or to do harm on the Sabbath?". Jesus touches on what is essential, he goes back to the central certainties that a small-minded casuistry loses from sight. This is the gift of counsel: *to know how to orientate oneself in the moral complexity of life.* St Thomas Aquinas writes, "The gift of counsel is the practical recall to the reasons of faith in our acting". And he adds, "To the sons of God is given the gift of counsel as their reason is instructed by the Holy Spirit on the actions that are to be accomplished".

II – THE GIFT OF COUNSEL IN THE CHRISTIAN

The gift of counsel is therefore extremely necessary for the Christian, for two reasons in particular.

• We noted above that often human situations are confused. Good and evil find themselves mixed together, each reality can be understood from diverse points of view which lead to diverse evaluations. This is the first reason why the Christian has need of an interior 'sureness', and of the freedom of the children, that helps to perceive with a sort of aesthetic sense what corresponds to the will of the Father, to the design of God.

How many occasions for seeking the will of God present themselves in personal life, in the life of couples, in family life and in the life of community! And also in political and public life.

How can one marry, for example, the defence of morality with a law that must at the same time take into account the consensus of a majority? How can one act so that a law does not favour evil and at the same time does not take away freedom? How many difficult choices there are for legislators regarding marriage, divorce, abortion, homosexual couples, a just concept of the family, the war against drugs, the dilemma between a welfare state and economic viability, and so on. How difficult it is to evaluate the pros and the cons in the various measures that are taken concerning the common good!

• There is a second reason that makes the gift of counsel extremely necessary. Often because of the complexity of life we are unsure and doubtful, even anguished, when faced by certain serious decisions.

The gift of counsel allows us to see all in the light of eternity and in what God the good Father desires. Thus it placates anguish, restores peace of heart and gives a clarity in action.

Again Thomas Aquinas wrote a pregnant phrase: thanks to the gift of counsel in our acting "sedatur anxietas dubitationis"; that is, our anxiety of doubt which was making us continually postpone without arriving at any decision is relieved, calmed and soothed.

Many times it has happened to me that I come face to face with these paralysing doubts, particularly in young people who are confronted with important life decisions (what type of studies to undertake, what lifestyle to adopt, which person to share one's life with)!

Naturally the gift of counsel is not a magic one, but shows us a way to find light and peace, to make authentic decisions with courage without frittering away one's time in months and years of frustrating waiting. When one puts off decisions because one does not know what to do and prefers not to think about it, when one goes ahead under the illusion that sometime someone will tell you what to do, all this signifies that the gift of counsel is lacking.

Perhaps you know that in recent years I have accompanied more than a thousand young people on their vocational search, proposing to them an itinerary of a year of discernment in order to arrive at a greater clarity regarding their choices. I asked them, during the year, to undertake some ascetic exercises of prayer and reflection, and to keep two rules: to renounce television for a year and to banish from their hearts each anxiety and anguish about the future. Well, all agreed that they found the first rule easy enough to follow, and the second very difficult. This is because to banish anguish when faced by important decisions is a gift of the Spirit which must be invoked with faithfulness and perseverance.

At this point one could ask oneself, *are there rules and aids to prepare oneself to receive the gift of counsel?*

The spiritual tradition has in fact developed the so-called *Rules for the Discernment of Spirits,* which are still valid and pertinent. Not having the time to explain them all, I would like at least to underline the basic principle which is simple and almost unexpected: the *primacy of joy.* The Holy Spirit gives joy. It is necessary therefore to learn to distinguish between joy and sadness of heart, to evaluate the difference between superficial pleasure and profound joy, between authentic joy and its caricature. What is important however is that the principle remains that of joy, because the action of the Spirit, which enters into us with the gift of counsel, carries us towards true joy, towards serenity, towards a sincere enthusiasm and towards a clear and courageous way of acting.

This is the beauty of the gift of counsel: it forms personalities which are strong, tranquil and sure of themselves; while the action of the evil spirit leads us to sadness, to turning in on ourselves, to a confusion that blocks the mind, to an anxiety that lacerates us and impedes us from deciding, making us remain always at the same point.

III – THE GIFT OF KNOWLEDGE

The gift of knowledge is another gift which is linked to the virtue of faith, as the gift of counsel is. Together they help us to live our faith in the difficult circumstances of this world, and to profess our faith with liberty, joy and ease.

Today, 'knowledge'* is a venerable term, and when we say, 'the verdict of science', we

---

* The Italian word used to designate this gift could be translated into English as both 'science' and 'knowledge'. The Cardinal makes the point that science is often regarded today as being *the* source of knowledge.

mean to say that something cannot be argued with. The scientist is a little like the prophet of our days and, for many problems in medicine, in economics and in society we turn to science almost as with a request for salvation.

In reality, the meaning of the term 'knowledge' in the Scriptures is different. The same Hebrew word in Isaiah 11:2 – with which we began our meditations – "the spirit of knowledge and the fear of the Lord", refers above all to *knowledge of God*. The future Messiah will know the Lord, as the Bible often says: "Know that the Lord is God" (Ps 100:3); "For the earth will be full of the knowledge of the Lord as the waters cover the sea" (Is 11:9); "For I desire steadfast love and not sacrifice, the knowledge of God rather than burnt offerings" (Hos 6:6).

The knowledge which is the gift of the Spirit is the knowledge of God, and of created things in their relation to God.

It is therefore above all in this sense that one speaks of the spiritual gift of knowledge; that is, of the capacity to establish a link between God and all the things in the world, going beyond appearances and comprehending the symbolic and relative value of each creature in respect to the being and the mystery of God, and of him who created everything. The gift of knowledge is extremely important, and I would like to repeat the words that I used in my pastoral letter *Three Tales of the Spirit*: It is thanks to the gift of knowledge that the great theological systems in the history of the faith were born and Christianity is able to contribute to the research on questions concerning both ultimate meaning and present necessities, when faced by various types of cultural and ethical questions and challenges (the gift of knowledge has therefore a very great ethical and social importance). Thanks to the knowledge of faith it is possible to discern the signs of the times and the leaven of the Gospel present everywhere, even in situations apparently closed to the light of revealed truth. Thanks to knowledge it is possible to understand the concrete needs of a community and to outline an pastoral project appropriate for it.

We must not think, however, that the gift is reserved for scholars and the learned, even though it is necessary for them. It is a *baptismal gift* of all the faithful and often – as for the other gifts – one finds it in the more humble people.

Perhaps the most striking example is found in the figure of the saint Curé d'Ars, who was parish priest of a tiny village near Lyons in the last century. He was not very cultured nor very intelligent, but he attracted all of France to himself and knew how to explain the mysteries of God with extreme simplicity and profundity. He knew the needs of the people in depth and read their hearts. I will quote one of his sayings concerning the gift of knowledge:

A Christian moved by the Holy Spirit knows how to make the difference. The eye of the world does not see further than this life, just as my eyes do not see further than this wall when the doors of the church are closed. But the eye of the Christian sees into the depths of eternity.

The gift of knowledge was present in a particular way in the young Thérèse of the Child Jesus, the holy Carmelite nun who on 19 October (1997) will be declared by the Pope 'Doctor of the Church', that is to say, 'learned' in the knowledge of God: knowledgeable in and an authentic master of the things of God. She wrote the following in 1896, when she had already entered into the darkness of faith, into 'the night of the spirit':

Do not think that I am sailing in consolations. No! My consolation is to have none on the earth. Without showing himself, without my hearing his voice, Jesus teaches me deep down inside: not by means of books, because I do not understand that which I read, but sometimes I have found that a word comes to console me at the end of prayer (after having remained in silence and aridity), "Behold the master that I give, he will teach you everything that you must do. I want to make you read in the book of life, where is contained the science of love".

And she exclaims:

The science of love, oh yes! The word resounds sweetly in my soul, I desire only this knowledge. For this, having given all my riches, I think, like the spouse of the Canticles to not have given anything yet (*Autobiographical Manuscript B*).

We are invited to examine ourselves on the science of love and on the gift of counsel.

Three questions for a moment of silence

I want to suggest then, as before, three questions.

1. I have said that the *gift of counsel* is linked with inner happiness and joy. *What gives a profound and spiritual joy to me in my life?* What do I think of when I hear speak of the joy of

the heart? What moments and what dreams come to my mind?

In responding to this question we will learn to know ourselves and how much of our joy is that of the Holy Spirit, which stimulates us to act well and which instils serenity, certainty and solidity into our actions.

2. I have underlined the relationship between the *gift of counsel and the complexity of the present world* – an ethical, juridical, social and cultural complexity. Do these complexities scare me? Do I perhaps seek to escape them by constantly lamenting and deprecating, dreaming of a different world? Or do I search, with the help of the Spirit, to discern good where there is good in order to thank God and to welcome that good and promote it?

The gift of counsel stimulates us to seek for what is good because Christ is risen and lives in the midst of us, therefore it is he who suggests, supports, and promotes the good.

3. Bearing in mind that the *knowledge of God* is also the knowledge of the human person, and that there exists a knowledge possessed by the 'Gospel' person which is to be learnt and expressed in our lives, I ask myself: *Do I allow myself to be guided by the true knowledge of the human person, by the knowledge which lies in the Gospel?* And do I allow myself to be

guided by attitudes such as: praying for my enemies, knowing how to lose in order to gain, preferring liberality to gain, and disinterestedness to advantage (giving of course each one of these attitudes its correct value)?

This is the true knowledge of the human person, a Gospel anthropology. These are all aspects of the 'science' of the Gospel that the Holy Spirit communicates to us believers in order to bring a new person to life, a new creature that lives in the Spirit and the divine 'sonship' that lives in the certainty of eternity, looking to the future with faith and with hope.

Let us pray so that an abundance of all the gifts of the Holy Spirit come upon us.

5.
Gifts of the Spirit are Understanding and Fortitude

Today the 17th of October, Pope John Paul II begins his 20th year of pontificate and we are close to him in prayer invoking on him an abundance of the gifts of the Holy Spirit, in particular of the gifts of understanding and fortitude of which we will speak in this last meditation of our Exercises.

Understanding★ *(intelligence)* is a gift which is appreciated by all, which all would like to have, and which each one thinks they have more than other people. No one can say that it does not interest them. Understanding is so

★ The Italian words used here mean 'intellect' and 'intelligence'. They have these meanings also when translated into English, but in the case of this particular gift of the Holy Spirit we tend to use 'understanding' as it is more appropriate.

much part of our everyday world that attempts are even made to produce it artificially, i.e. as in artificial intelligence.

But what does one mean when, in listing the seven gifts, one mentions that of understanding, or intuition, or intelligence?

We will try to understand this gift together with the gift of fortitude (or strength). The idea of fortitude, particularly when expressed by the term 'strength', is currently in fashion. This is true above all when we talk about physical strength either for its own sake, or as an essential element of an attractive physical appearance. One speaks much about health as an absolute and indispensable value, one which is totally desirable. One speaks much about that elegant and refined version of physical strength which is fitness, the full possession of one's own physical capacities. One talks as well about political strength, military strength, or bargaining power. On the other hand, one hears much less about moral strength or strength of soul, which appears a rare commodity in this time of conformism.

And it is precisely this strength of soul, as a gift of the Spirit, that we would like to examine jointly with the gift of understanding in order to see how they are at work in Jesus and how they are given to Christians.

I – THE GIFT OF UNDERSTANDING IN JESUS AND IN CHRISTIANS

Here I quote two passages from the Gospel according to Luke. Jesus said,

> "The Son of Man must undergo great suffering, and be rejected by the elders, chief priests, and scribes, and be killed, and on the third day be raised." Then he said to them all, "If any want to become my followers, let them deny themselves and take up their cross daily and follow me" (Lk 9:22-23).

This first prediction of the Passion is followed by a second:

> And all were astounded at the greatness of God. While everyone was amazed at all that he was doing, he said to his disciples, "Let these words sink into your ears: The Son of Man is going to be betrayed into human hands." But they did not understand this saying; its meaning was concealed from them, so that they could not perceive it. And they were afraid to ask him about this (Lk 9:43-45).

1. First of all we read that the Son of Man *must* undergo great suffering. There is therefore a

divine mystery, a divine order to things that is not however – as sometimes has been believed – an almost perverse predestination (i.e. it is necessary at any cost that Jesus should suffer), but rather it is the consequence of love. Jesus lives totally for the Father, he lives totally for other people and he intuits clearly where, in an evil world, to bring his love. The 'must' indicates the profound intuition that Jesus had about what was to happen to him, living in total dedication to the Father and to people in a world of sin. *He must undergo great suffering.* And this is repugnant to human beings, to each one of us.

And not only suffer, but *be rejected.* This is a suffering which touches all the dimensions of the person: not to feel oneself accepted, to feel oneself disliked, and cast out from society. And this rejection does not come just from anybody, but from the civil and religious authorities – that is, Elders, High Priests and Scribes. It appears that for Jesus there is truly no space for him to live.

Finally, *to be put to death,* rejected to the point of being eliminated.

And then to rise, which is the thing that turns everything upside down.

Let us contemplate in the words of Jesus his understanding of the mystery of God which is love until death and the victory of life in death. Jesus intuits, understands all of this to the very core. His is a gift, an attitude of profound understanding of the mysteries of God, of humankind and of history.

2. Seeing this clarity of understanding in Jesus we note by comparison how much the disciples are struggling to comprehend – how moreover there is present in them the will not to comprehend, and this shows itself in their being afraid to even address their questions to him.

The two passages from Luke show therefore a contrast between two attitudes: on one hand, there is the intuition that Jesus has of his destiny, of the mystery of the kingdom, of the mystery of love right until death, and of the mystery of victory of life over death; on the other hand, there is the lack of understanding, the resistance of human beings to this understanding and even the resistance of the disciples.

We might ask ourselves, why is there such great resistance? The explanation is given us in verse 23 of the Gospel text: "If any want to become my followers, let them deny themselves and take up their cross daily and follow me".

We realise, if we were to enter into this intuition of Jesus, into the mystery of love, of the Cross and of death, we will have to take a path similar to his, we will have to take up the Cross every day and follow him. For this reason we unconsciously resist spiritual understanding. We would prefer not to have it, not to know, and to go on our way in blindness. And yet such an understanding is a great gift and we have great need of it.

• We have great need of it in order to understand the divine mysteries, the relation between the Cross and the Trinity, between the Cross and the Fatherhood of God. We have need of it in order to intuit in this divine mystery that of our own life and death. Without such a gift, we will not be able to look ahead with courage in life.

• We have need of it in order to understand how the mystery of God is revealed in our time, in order to understand how it is hidden in our time, hidden and yet we can find it; in order to understand how Jesus crucified and risen lives amongst us and how we can meet him; in order to understand how the Holy Spirit is at work in the midst of us and how we can let ourselves be brought to life and be revived by him.

This understanding of our time, which is visited and loved by God, is extremely important in order not to lose heart when faced with the phenomena of secularism and religious indifference, phenomena that seem to make our society very arid.

We could say, using an image, that the understanding of the mysteries of God in our time is the gift to discover the gardens, the green spaces, the tufts of grass that grow amongst the stones; and to give to them air, water and the sun's light, so that they might grow the better and might give us joy and change the worn face of our society.

Summing up, the gift of spiritual understanding is fundamental to give clarity, strength and serenity to our actions, to enable us to discover among the folds of daily life the presence of the Father, the Son, the Holy Spirit, to enable us to contemplate in our own crosses the presence of the Risen One.

II – THE GIFT OF FORTITUDE IN JESUS AND IN CHRISTIANS

Hand in hand with the gift of understanding comes also the gift of fortitude, moral strength, strength of soul, the last of the gifts on which we will meditate.

1. The gift of fortitude in Jesus appears above all in his attitude when faced by death.

It was now about noon, and darkness came over the whole land until three in the afternoon, while the sun's light failed; and the curtain of the temple was torn in two. Then Jesus, crying with a loud voice, said, "Father, into your hands I commend my spirit." Having said this, he breathed his last (Lk 23:44-46).

At the death of Jesus there was a great darkness on the earth, all was shrouded in anguish and fear; the veil of the temple was torn, that is to say the securities of human institutions tumbled, and Jesus looked death in the face with a cry of trusting abandonment. Even in the face of death he lives the mystery of the Father, of fatherhood, in whose hands is his life.

The *fortitude of Jesus is his victory over the fear of death* and of every other evil, because he knows himself to be in the arms of the Father who will never abandon him.

2. This is the meaning of the gift of fortitude or strength of soul for Christians. The *fortitude is the gift which gives us the capacity to confess our faith even amidst contradictions and dangers.* And the outstanding instance of the gift of fortitude is *martyrdom*, the overcoming of the fear of death because one knows oneself to be in the hand of God.

St Ambrose loved the Martyrs greatly. For this he is buried here, beside the two Martyrs Gervasius and Protasius. He valued fortitude as an immense gift, as the source of the ancient greatness (of the two Martyrs) which he wished to have at his side.

The gift of fortitude perfects the virtue of hope taking it as far as heroism, as the despising of death, as the overcoming of the fear of death.

We will never be able to pray enough to have the gifts of understanding and of strength of soul that are given to us in prayer.

Let us listen in this respect to Thérèse of the Child of Jesus, written in pencil in the final months of her life:

> A wise man said, "Give me a lever, something to lean on and I will raise the world". That which Archimedes was not able to obtain, because he did not address his request to God and expressed his request only from a material point of view, the saints have obtained fully. The Omnipotent has given them as a point on which to lean, *himself and himself alone;* as a lever, *the prayer which burns with a flame of love,* and thus they have raised the world; thus the saints of the Church militant raised it, and future saints will also raise it, right until the end of the world (*Autobiographical Manuscript C*).

This is the prayer which obtains understanding and fortitude: Be strong in the Lord, as St

Paul teaches in his letter to the Ephesians, "Finally, be strong in the Lord and in the strength of his power" (Eph 6:10).

This is a fortitude which is very necessary for us in order to profess ourselves Christian in a hostile environment and in an indifferent world. We know that the greatest temptation for a young person, for an adolescent who is faced by life, is the fear to behave in a way which is different from the group, to be derided by their companions and not to do as the others do. This explains the abandonment, the desertions and the flight of many young people from the *oratorio*.* They do not have the courage or the strength to go against the current.

For this reason, all of us need the gift of fortitude and we are invited to ask for it in prayer, for ourselves and for other people.

The strength of soul moreover is especially necessary in the trials of life, in the sufferings, in illnesses, in losses – when, that is to say, our weakness seems to be an insuperable object. In this regard, I would like to quote more words from Christina, the young woman who died of cancer at 26 years of age, of whom I have already spoken to you. She writes in her diary:

---

* A form of youth club in Italy, which is attached to a parish.

Jesus, I am not able to sustain you on the Cross because I do not feel you anymore. However, take my fears and my wretched state, and save somebody, thus all this will not be in vain. I offer you these things even if in this moment I do not feel you. *I know that you are there* and even if I am not able to manage, I will try to find the strength.

It is in hearing words such as these of Christina, words from our own time, that we are able to exclaim, "The Holy Spirit with his gifts of understanding and strength is truly present today, in many people!".

Concluding reflections

We have come to the end of our evenings together and I would like to thank you for your presence in the Basilica of St Ambrose and also for the presence of the innumerable hearts united with us through radio and television. I have felt, thanks to you, the refreshing and life-giving breath of the Spirit of God.

I would like to conclude with three reflections, which have grown inside me during these days.

The first is an objection: We speak so much about the Spirit, but where is he?

The second is the question: What provides the unifying factor between the seven gifts of the Spirit (and further, why 'seven')?

The third is an observation, the final word with which I leave you because it could also be the fruit of our Exercises.

1. *The objection.* Each evening, while returning home, after having spoken to you, I noticed that a difficulty was growing inside of me and perhaps grew also in you: If there truly are the gifts of the Spirit, how come *actions of Christians are so weak, uncertain and incoherent?* How come there is so much need to ask forgiveness for our historical failings – as the Pope has done – if there is the Spirit?

Here we come to the very nub of the Exercises. If in fact we have completed the Exercises, perhaps we begin to perceive that it is precisely in this state of agonised conscience that many Christians do without the Holy Spirit. They do not bother about his movements, about his invitations, they do not trust themselves to his gifts and they do not recognise them in their lives.

This is the great suffering of the Church: that the Holy Spirit, so rich in gifts, should be the great *unknown*, not from a doctrinal point of view but rather from a practical point of view. Many people – perhaps often us as well – act upon their own account, they count on their own strengths, and they think to have all in hand. And then the gifts of the Spirit do not show themselves, they remain inert and stifled.

As a first fruit of our evenings, I wish that each one of us might be able to *realise and to become aware that we have the gifts of the Spirit,* and that a spiritual Christianity is a Christianity which allows itself to be moved not by human reasons, by social and political convenience, but rather by the Spirit of God. This is the meaning of the whole of my pastoral letter, *Three Tales of the Holy Spirit*: that we let ourselves be moved by the gifts, not that we expect to *feel* we have fortitude or understanding or wisdom; let us not allow ourselves to 'stall', thinking that we lack such things. But let us neither throw ourselves into action, almost as if all were to depend on us! Let us invoke the Spirit and move ourselves in the certainty that he will come to help us in our weakness.

I would truly like that from these Exercises there might be born the consciousness of a *spiritual Christianity,* whose basic motive force is the Spirit of Jesus risen.

2. The second question: Is there a word or a concept which provides the unifying factor between the seven gifts?

Certainly. All are gifts of the Spirit that

make us children in the Son Jesus. The unifying factor is therefore the *divine Fatherhood*, is the being children of God in Jesus – but in fullness, in joy, in creativity and enthusiasm. We participate then in the wisdom, understanding, counsel, strength of soul, fear of God, knowledge and the piety of Jesus, realising that we also are children of God and that in Jesus we can address ourselves to the Father. Then we will be able to see all things in relation to him, with wisdom. We will move with ease, strength and understanding amongst all the things of this world, seeing in them a gift from the Father and a way to the Father. All the riches of knowledge, of piety, and fear of God, which are conceded to the children, come from this relationship.

The summary of all this, for that reason, can be expressed with the prayer *Our Father.*

3. *The third reflection, as a final fruit of the Exercises, is to have a noble, great, high idea of the Christian life according to the Spirit.*

The Baptismal life, with the virtues of faith, hope and charity and with the gifts of wisdom, understanding, strength of soul and so on, that accompany these fundamental attitudes of existence (the virtues of faith, hope and charity), is not a life that is mediocre, or drags along, or is sad, or is half illuminated; it is instead a life that is dignified,

rich, joyful, free, always new and fresh, attentive to other people and attentive to God
without forgetting the others. And it is, in
fact, the only proposal for a life which is rich
and full that the world of today really knows
how to offer. It is so because it is the very life
of Jesus in us and the life of the Spirit that
made St Ambrose great, and that made great
a small and humble soul like Thérèse of the
Child Jesus. It is the life in the Spirit which
calls each one of us to a greatness of soul and
to a nobility of existence.

This is the life that we wish for each other,
with which we want to serve society, placing
in it the new strength of the Spirit, for the
advantage of all. It was the pastoral dream of
Ambrose that is still the pastoral dream of our
Church: we would wish that this strength,
understanding, wisdom, knowledge, counsel,
the fear of God and piety could be commu-
nicated to all.

Let us pray intensely so that the flame of
the Spirit burns not only in our own hearts,
but that it might warm and illuminate of
those who live in our society.

Appendix
Decalogue for an Examination of Conscience of the Community

To the following examination of conscience I would like to call all our communities – parishes, associations, groups, movements – so that they might submit themselves willingly and with generosity to the judgement of the Word of God and that they might open themselves to the breath of the Spirit.

1. *Be a community of faith, nourished by the faith of all the Church alive in an unconditional adhesion of heart and of life to the living God who has spoken to you in Jesus Christ! Cultivate an up-rightness of intention, be joyful in affliction, quick in mercy towards those who are near and far away!*
   Is your faith that of the Catholic Church? Do you live intensely your adhesion to the

living God and the Church that he made you encounter? Are you a community that listens to the Word with faith, that celebrates the divine liturgy and witnesses to the Gospel of the Lord Jesus? How do you live the Beatitude of the poor of heart, of the afflicted, and of the merciful?

2. *Submit yourself to the Word of God in interior prayer and in communion with your pastors, in order to be a community rich in spiritual understanding, and capable of holding things together in unity in the midst of the fragmentation and confusion of our time!*

How do you live spiritual understanding? Are you quick to submit yourself to the Word of God? Do you let yourself be questioned by it? In the inner life of your community are you a 'school of prayer' and of *lectio divina*? Do you hold sincerely to the magisterium of the pastors? Do you measure the understanding given to you in your charism and to the masters amongst you against the understanding of the Catholic faith and against the guidance to understanding of the Scriptures which is offered by the Pope and your bishop?

3. *Be a community desirous of growing in the understanding of the faith, nourished by dependable masters, that you might be voices in the*

*symphony of the truth that illuminates and saves
– the truth which is present in the variety and richness of witness given to the entire Catholic communion, in time and in space, in the past and in the
present! Be a community that conceives and carries
out a pastoral plan in faithfulness to the Spirit!*

In all our communities it is necessary to
open oneself to the gift of the Holy Spirit,
in communion with all the Church: are you
a community that nourishes itself on the
knowledge of the faith? Do you take care of
the catechetical and theological formation
of your members? Do you bother to listen
to the masters of theology and of spiritual
experience, that the Spirit raises up in the
Church and which she proposes to you or
recommends? Are you attentive to pastoral
projects?

4. *Be a community docile to the gift of counsel,
respectful towards the personal paths of spiritual
growth! Be ready to help each one to live in liberty
their own choices under the action of the Consoler
and the guide of people who are wise and interiorly
free!*

Are you a community where the gift of
counsel is appreciated and promoted? Are
the itineraries of personal growth and of
conscience, respected and valued amongst
you, even when they are difficult for the
community as a whole on its journey? Do

you encourage your members in the practice of spiritual direction, undertaken with people who should be sufficiently free with respect to the temptation to absolutise membership of a certain group? Do you realise that your movement or group is 'a way', one of the many ways in the Church? That this 'way' is truly of the Church only when it recognises that there are also 'other ways' and they can be vocations from God, and without all of these the plan of salvation, in the today of the Church, is not complete?

5. *Be a community alive in hope, able to always witness to all the overflowing goodness of the promises of God! The God who liberates us from every prison of present evils and from the fear of death, and makes us look ahead with faith, with detachment from earthly goods and from money, with a certainty that is stronger than every failure or persecution or defeat!*

Are you a community rich in hope? Before the many evils of the present time, do you keep at a high level the ability to always, and no matter what happens, look ahead to the horizon of the future which God has for us? Do you witness to hope to whoever meets you? Do you live the joy of those who hope in the Lord? Do you live the beatitude of the poor in spirit, of those who hunger for justice and of the persecuted?

6. *Be a community that lives under the gaze of God, desiring to please him alone in all things! For this reason watchful and hard-working in the fear of his holy name, free from evaluations and calculations of a merely worldly nature!*

What place do you give to the fear of God in your evaluations and in your projects? Are you a community that allows itself to be judged by the Lord, preoccupied to please him in everything? Do you measure yourself by the demands of the Gospel and by the following of Jesus or do you allow yourself sometimes to be bewitched by plans for earthly success?

7. *Be a community strong in hope, persevering in the path that God has marked out for you and the Church has confirmed through its pastors, free and courageous in faithfulness and in witness, even when it costs! Be liberating for all the members of your community and for whoever draws close to you, in the gift of true freedom which comes from the Lord!*

Are you a community strong in hope? Are you constant in your paths, persevering in your faithfulness to the call of God? Are you reliable? Do you keep yourself faithful to the tasks you have undertaken, even if these were to cost you and to request of you sacrifices which are not indifferent?

8. Be a community alive and hard-working in charity, open, capable of concrete gestures of reconciliation, welcoming and generous towards all your brothers and sisters in the faith, even if they are different from you! Be quick to allow space to another person, whoever they might be and from wherever they might come, in order to receive them with respect and love and to offer them freely the gift which God has given you! Forgive with joy, work with all your strength, for the peacefulness of hearts!

Are you an open community? Are you welcoming and generous? Are you respectful towards the diversity that exists within the Church, not only in word, but with facts and in truth? And are you open and welcoming to whoever from outside draws near to you, especially with those who seek the face of God and desire to meet Jesus Christ? Are you quick to make use of the Church to serve your own ends, or do you serve her, so that the Kingdom of God might grow, even if you must grow less? How great is your meekness when faced by incomprehension and offences? How do you help understanding and peace?

9. Be a community rich in piety, in love with God and desirous of responding to his love with a humble love, but tender, passionate and disposed to keep him company in his sorrow and in his joy in every moment!

A community of faith, of hope and of charity can be recognised in a particular way by its piety. Are you a community striving to adore and venerate God in every choice? Do you nourish in your members this tenderness for God, which is the fruit of a great love, received from on high and given freely? Do you witness in this world to the urgency of loving the Lord above all, with all our heart, with all our mind, with all our being?

10. *Be a community rich in spiritual wisdom, able to evaluate and to live everything placing it under the primacy of charity, which comes from God and makes us participants in the life of God: make your way to him and to his infinite love, rather than making your way in this world!*

Are you a community that lives the wisdom of love and the wisdom of the Cross? Do you make the primacy of charity real in all things? Do you allow yourselves to be loved by God in order that each member of your community might be welcoming and generous in love?

Book II

The Gifts
of the Holy Spirit

DOM PROSPER GUÉRANGER

Foreword

Compared to the first book by Martini this second book by Guéranger presents a few problems for a present-day reader. The work was written well over 100 years ago and uses language and ideas that are not always easy for people today to understand or accept. Guéranger belonged to a time when Catholicism generally expressed itself in a more severe and authoritative way than it is necessarily inclined to do today. This goes for spiritual matters as much as for anything else. When Guéranger was writing, the Church was less open to an understanding of the ambiguities involved in human experience than we are now, thanks, for instance, to the insights gained through psychology. Furthermore, Guéranger explains the gifts from a more doctrinal point of view.

In writing the way he did he would have considered that he stood securely within the centuries-old spiritual tradition of Catholic

Christianity. To this tradition he is certainly a witness. The harsh tone he adopts towards sinful and erring humanity is quite faithful to this tradition – though other witnesses such as Francis de Sales would give a different impression, and the tone adopted by Guéranger might have been considered unhelpful by some of his own contemporaries. If, however, we examine our own lives honestly we might be more inclined to try and understand the thoughts he expresses regarding the miserable state and evil actions of confirmed sinners! Take, for instance, the "sad inconsistency" discussed on pages 115-116. We should at least have some insight into what Guéranger is talking about. There can't be many who haven't in some way compromised their commitment to God or betrayed their own dearly-held beliefs.

We should not allow themselves to be confused (or even discouraged) by the very real differences between the Catholic mentality of Guéranger's time and that of ours. The reader who perseveres will discover in Guéranger a genuine witness to the riches of the spiritual tradition which exists in the Catholic Church.

Introduction: The Gifts of the Holy Spirit

The gifts of the Holy Spirit are seven energies which the Holy Spirit himself consents to place in our souls, when he enters into them with sanctifying grace. Actual graces put into motion simultaneously or separately these powers which have been divinely instilled in us, and the praiseworthy and supernatural good of eternal life is produced with the consent of our will.

The prophet Isaiah, guided by divine inspiration, has made these seven gifts known to us. In the passage where he describes the working of the Holy Spirit in the soul of the Son of God made man, whom he represents to us as a shoot sprung from the virginal trunk of Jesse, he tells us:

> The Spirit of the Lord shall rest on him,
> the spirit of wisdom and understanding,
> the spirit of counsel and might, the spirit

101

of knowledge and piety; and the spirit of the fear of the Lord will fill him (Is 11:2,3 – Greek and Latin versions).

There is nothing more mysterious than these words. But one feels in what they are trying to express, that one is not dealing with a simple enumeration of the characteristics of the Holy Spirit, but rather with a description of the effects which he produces in the human soul. Thus it was understood in the Christian tradition found in the writings of the ancient Fathers, and thus it has been formulated by theological reflection.

The sacred humanity of the incarnate Son of God is the supernatural type of our own humanity. That which the Spirit has worked in the sacred humanity to sanctify it, has to take place in us in a way proportionate to this nature of ours. He placed in the Son of Mary the seven energies that the prophet describes; the same gifts are prepared for human beings once regenerated. One must take note of the importance of their sequence. Isaiah names first the spirit of wisdom, and then descends, finishing with the spirit of fear of God. Wisdom is in effect, as we will see, the highest of all the privileges to which the human soul could be elevated, while the fear of God, according to the profound expression of the Psalmist, is only the beginning and the early stages of this divine quality. It is easily understandable how the soul of Jesus, called to enter into a personal union with the Word, should have been treated with particular dignity, in such a way that the gift of wisdom would have been infused in his soul as an essential quality, while the gift of the fear of God, a necessary quality in a created nature, would only have been placed in his divine nature as a complementary one. For us, on the other hand, fragile and inconstant as we are, the fear of God is the foundation of the entire structure, and it is through this gift that we ascend by degrees to that wisdom which unites us to God. Human beings therefore, rise to perfection by means of the gifts of the Holy Spirit using them in an order which is the reverse of that which Isaiah laid out for the incarnate Son of God. And these gifts are conferred on them in baptism, and are restored to them in the sacrament of reconciliation if they have had the misfortune to lose grace because of mortal sin.

Let us admire with profound respect these august seven whose mark one finds impressed on all the works of our salvation and of our sanctification. Seven virtues render the soul pleasing to God. Thanks to seven gifts, the Holy Spirit leads the soul to perfection. Seven sacraments communicate to it the fruits of the incarnation and of the redemption of

Jesus Christ. Finally, it is after seven weeks have passed from Easter that the Spirit is sent on the earth in order to establish and consolidate the Kingdom of God there. We must not be astonished if, after all this, Satan has tried to sacrilegiously parody the divine work, opposing to it the horrendous seven of the capital vices, with which he endeavours to lead astray the person whom God wants to save.

1.

The Gift of the Fear of God

The obstacle to the good in us is pride. It is pride that induces us to resist God, to place our end in ourselves, in a word to go astray and lose ourselves. Only humility can save us from such a great danger. Who will give us humility? The Holy Spirit, diffusing in us the gift of the fear of God.

This sentiment is based on a conviction given to us by faith. This conviction tells us of the Majesty of God, in whose presence we are nothing, and of his infinite sanctity, before which we are nothing other than unworthiness and defilement. The conviction tells us of his sovereignly just judgement which he must exercise over us when we leave this life, and of a fall which is always possible if we fail to respond to the grace which never fails us, but which we can resist.

The salvation of the human person is worked out therefore 'with fear and trembling', as the Apostle teaches us (Phil 2:12). But this fear, which is a gift of the Holy Spirit, is not a coarse sentiment that might satisfy itself with casting us into terror at the thought of eternal punishments. It keeps us in compunction of heart, even though our sins have long been forgiven. It prevents us from forgetting that we are sinners, that we owe all to divine mercy, and that we are saved only in hope (Rom 8:24).

This fear of God is not therefore a servile fear. It becomes, on the contrary, the source of the most delicate sentiments. It can ally itself to love, being nothing more than a filial sentiment that fears sin because of the offence that it gives to God. Inspired by respect for the divine Majesty, by the sentiment of his infinite sanctity, it puts creatures in their true place, and St Paul teaches us that, thus purified, they contribute to "making (our) holiness perfect in the fear of God" (2 Cor 7:1). We also hear this great Apostle, who had been caught up into the third heaven, confess that he is rigorous towards himself, "so that after proclaiming to others I myself should not be disqualified" (1 Cor 9:27).

The spirit of independence and of false liberty which reigns today, helps to render more scarce the fear of God, and this is one of the plagues of our time. A false familiarity with God too often substitutes this fundamental disposition of the Christian life, and when this happens, every progress comes to a halt, illusion enters the soul, and the sacraments, which at the moment of return to God had acted with great force, become almost sterile. The fact is that the gift of fear has been smothered by the vain satisfaction that the soul finds in itself. Humility is extinguished; a secret and universal pride has come to paralyse the movement of this soul. The soul, without realising it, is reduced to not knowing God anymore, precisely because it does not tremble anymore before him.

Preserve in us, therefore, O divine Spirit, the gift of the fear of God that you have diffused in us at our baptism. This salutary fear will assure our perseverance in good, halting the progress of the spirit of pride. May it be as a dart that passes right through our souls. May it remain fixed there for ever, as our safeguard. May it bring us down from our lofty pinnacles, pull us out of our weakness, and reveal to us without ceasing the greatness and the sanctity of him who created us and who must judge us.

We know, O divine Spirit, that this blessed fear does not suffocate love. Far from doing so, it eliminates the obstacles that would halt the development of love. The celestial Powers see and love with ardour the highest Good, they are rapt up into it for eternity; and nevertheless they tremble before his terrible Majesty: *tremunt Potestates*. And we, covered with the scars of sin, full of imperfections, exposed to a thousand hidden dangers, constrained to struggle against many enemies, should we not perhaps feel that we must stimulate with a great fear – which is at the same time filial – our will that so easily falls asleep, and our spirit that so many darknesses besiege? Watch over your work, O divine Spirit, preserve in us the precious gift that you deigned to give us. Teach us to reconcile peace and joy of heart with the fear of God, according to the warning of the psalmist: "Serve the Lord with fear, and rejoice in him with trembling" (Ps 2:11 – Latin and Greek versions).

2.
The Gift of Piety

The gift of the fear of God is destined to cure in us the plague of pride. The gift of piety is diffused in our souls by the Holy Spirit in order to combat self-centredness and egoism, which is one of the wicked passions of the fallen human being and the second obstacle to their union with God. Christians' hearts must be neither cold nor indifferent. It is necessary that they be tender and open, otherwise they would not be able to ascend along the path onto which God, who is love, graciously deigned to call them.

The Holy Spirit produces therefore in human beings the gift of piety, inspiring in them a filial return to their creator: "You have received a spirit of adopted sons – the Apostle tells us – through which we cry, 'Abba! Father!'" (Rom 8:15). This disposition renders the soul sensitive to all that touches on the honour of God. It helps persons nourish in themselves a compunction for their own sins at the sight of the infinite goodness which graciously condescended to bear with them and to forgive them, and at the thought of the sufferings and of the death of the Redemptor. The soul initiated in the gift of piety desires the glory of God constantly. It would like to lead all human beings to his feet, and the outrages which God receives are particularly distressing for it. Its joy consists in seeing the progress of souls in love, and the devotion that this love inspires in them for him who is the Highest good. Full of a filial submission to this universal Father who is in heaven, piety is ready to do whatever he wills. It resigns itself from its heart to every ordering of his Providence.

The soul's faith is simple and alive. It submits lovingly to the Church, always ready to renounce its own most deeply held ideas, if they were to deviate in some way from her teaching or practice, having an instinctive horror of novelty and independence.

This devotion to God which the gift of piety inspires, uniting the soul to its creator through filial affection, unites it with fraternal affection to all creatures, because they are the work of the power of God and they belong to God.

The first place in the love of the Christian, animated by the gift of piety, is occupied by the glorified creatures in whom God eternally takes his delight, and who rejoice in him for ever. The Christian loves Mary tenderly, and is jealous of her honour. They venerate the Saints with love. They admire with enthusiasm the courage of the Martyrs, and the heroic acts of virtue made by the friends of God. They delight in their miracles and honour their holy relics religiously.

But this affection is not directed solely at the creatures who are crowned in heaven. Those who are still in this world occupy a very great place in the Christian's heart. The gift of piety helps them find Jesus himself in these creatures. Their benevolence towards their brothers and sisters is universal. Their heart is disposed to the pardoning of injuries, to tolerance towards the imperfections of others, and to the excusing of all the wrongs of their neighbour. They show themselves compassionate towards the poor and attentive towards the sick. An affectionate sweetness reveals what is in the depths of their heart; and in their relations with their brothers and sisters on earth, one sees them always disposed to weep with those who weep and to rejoice with those who are joyful.

Such, O divine Spirit, is the disposition of those who cultivate the gift of piety that you have poured into their souls. Thanks to this ineffable benefit, you neutralise the perfidious egoism that would dry up their hearts, you liberate them from that hateful aridity that renders the human being indifferent towards its brothers and sisters, and you close their souls to envy and hatred. In order to obtain all this, nothing other is needed than this filial piety towards the creator. This piety renders their hearts tender, and their hearts are dissolved in a living affection for all that which has come from the hands of God. Make this very precious gift bear fruit in us. Do not permit that it be suffocated by a love for ourselves. Jesus has encouraged us, telling us that his heavenly father "makes his sun rise on the good and on the bad" (Mt 5:45). Do not permit, divine Paraclete, that such fatherly indulgence be wasted on us. Deign to make this seed of devotion, of benevolence, and of compassion – which you placed in our souls in the moment when you took possession of them through Holy Baptism – grow in us.

3.

The Gift of Knowledge

The soul, which has been removed from evil by the fear of God and opened to the noble affections by the gift of piety, experiences the need to know by what means it will be able to avoid the object of its fear, and how it will be able to find that which it must love. The Holy Spirit comes to help it, and gives it what it desires, infusing into it the gift of knowledge. Through this precious gift, the truth appears to it, it knows what God asks of it and that which he disapproves of, what it must seek out and that which it must flee. Without divine knowledge, we are in danger of losing sight of our way because of the darkness which too often obscures human knowledge, either in part or in full. This darkness comes first of all from our own depths which bear the all too real marks of decadence. It is caused, moreover, by the prejudices and maxims of the world which every day seduce or fool the spirits which one would think are the most upright. Finally, it comes from the activity of Satan, who is the Prince of Darkness and exerts himself largely with the aim of surrounding our souls with darkness, or to lead them astray with false lights.

The faith which has been infused into us at baptism is the light of our souls. Through the gift of knowledge, the Holy Spirit provides this virtue with rays that are bright enough to dissipate our darkness. Doubts then clear, error disappears and the truth appears in all its brilliance. One sees each thing in its true light, which is the light of faith. One discovers the deplorable errors that are diffused in the world, that seduce such a great number of souls. Errors, of which we ourselves might have been the victim for a long time.

The gift of knowledge reveals to us the end which God intended for creation, outside of which beings are able to find neither good nor repose. It teaches us the use to which we must put creatures, which have been given to us not so that they might be a stumbling block, but so they might help us on the way towards God. The secret of life thus being shown to us, our way becomes sure, we do not hesitate any more, and we feel inclined to distance ourselves from all paths that do not bring us to our destination.

It was this knowledge, gift of the Holy Spirit, which St Paul had in mind when, speaking to the Christians of Ephesus, he said to them, "Once you were darkness, but now in the Lord you are light. Live as children of light" (Eph 5:8). This is the source of the firmness and assurance of Christian conduct. Experience can sometimes be found wanting, and the world frets itself at the thought of false steps that it fears to take; but the world has not taken the gift of knowledge into account: "The Lord guides the just person on straight paths; and gives them the knowledge of the saints" (cf Wis 10:10). This lesson is given every day.

The Christian, by means of this supernatural light, escapes all dangers, and if they do not have their own experience, they have the experience of God.

May you be blessed, O divine Spirit, for this light which you diffuse in us, and which you conserve in us with such a loving perseverance. Never allow us to search for another light. This light alone is sufficient for us. Outside of it there is only darkness. Preserve us from the sad inconsistency into which many imprudently allow themselves to fall, accepting one day your guidance, and abandoning themselves the next to the prejudices of the world, leading a double life that satisfies neither the world nor you. We need, therefore, the love of this knowledge that you have given to us so that we might be saved; the enemy of our souls is jealous when he sees this salutary knowledge in us, and would like to substitute it with his shadows. Do not permit, divine Spirit, that he should succeed in his perfidious design, and help us always to discern that which is true from that which is false, and that which is just from that which is unjust. May our 'eye' be simple, according to the word of Jesus, so that all our body, that is to say, all of our actions, our desires and our thoughts as a whole, may be light (Mt 6:23). Save us from that 'eye' which Jesus calls unhealthy, and which makes the whole body full of darkness.

4.
The Gift of Fortitude

The gift of knowledge has taught us what we must do and what we must avoid in order to conform to the design of Jesus Christ, our divine head. Now it is necessary that the Holy Spirit establish in us a principle from which we can draw the energy needed to sustain us on the way which he has shown us. We must, in effect, take into account certain obstacles, and the great number of those who succumb should be sufficient to convince us of the need we have to be helped. The help that the Holy Spirit communicates to us is the gift of fortitude, through which, if we are faithful in employing it, it will be possible and even easy to triumph over all that could check us on our way.

In the difficulties and trials of life, human beings are sometimes brought to weakness and despondency, and sometimes urged on by a natural ardour that has its source in the person's temperament or in vanity. This dual disposition would do little to speed victory in the battles that the soul must fight for its own salvation. The Holy Spirit, therefore, supplies a new factor, a supernatural fortitude. This fortitude is so much part of the Spirit's nature, that, when the Saviour instituted his sacraments, one of them was specially created (Confirmation) to give us this divine Spirit as a source of energy and strength. It is beyond doubt that having to struggle during this life against the devil, the world and ourselves, we need something other than pusillanimity or boldness in order to resist. We need a gift that might restrain fear in us and at the same time temper the trust that we might place in ourselves. Those so modified by the Holy Spirit will conquer with certainty, because grace will compensate in them for the weakness of nature, and at the same time will correct their ardour.

In a Christian's life two necessities meet. They must know how to resist and how to endure. What could they oppose to the temptations of Satan, if the fortitude of the divine Spirit were not to come and cover them with heavenly armour and to arm their arm? Is the world not also a terrible adversary, if we consider the number of victims that it claims each day by the tyranny of its maxims, claims and pretensions? What mustn't the assistance of the divine Spirit be, when it is a question of making Christians invulnerable to the murderous darts that make a great slaughter around them?

The passions of a person's heart are by no means a minor obstacle to their salvation and their sanctification: an obstacle more fearful as it is more intimate. It is necessary that the Spirit transform the heart, that it even induce it to renounce itself when the heavenly light shows a way that is different from that towards which the love and pursuit of ourselves drives us. What divine fortitude isn't necessary in order to "hate your own life" (Jn 12:25), when Jesus demands it, and when it is a question of choosing between two masters whose service is incompatible (Mt 6:24)? The Holy Spirit works these wonders every day by means of the gift which he has diffused in us, if we do not despise this gift or stifle it in our cowardice or our imprudence. He teaches Christians to master their own passions, not to allow themselves to be led by these blind guides, not to yield to their instincts unless they are in conformity with the order that God has established.

Sometimes this divine Spirit does not only ask that Christians resist interiorly the enemies of their souls, it demands that they protest openly against the error of evil, if the duties of their state, or their position demand it. Then it is necessary to brave that type of unpopularity of which Christians are at times victim, but this must not surprise them, when they remember the words of the Apostle, "If I were still pleasing people, I would not be a servant of Christ" (Gal 1:10). But the Spirit is never to be found lacking, and when he meets a soul that is resolved to use the divine fortitude of which he is the source, not only does the Spirit assure it of the triumph, but normally he places the soul in a state of peace which is full of sweetness and courage, and which comes from the victory over the passions.

This is the way in which the Holy Spirit applies the gift of fortitude to Christians when they must practice resistance. We have said that this precious gift produces at the same time the energy necessary to endure the trials which are the price of salvation. There are certain fears which freeze the courage and can bring a person to perdition. The gift of fortitude dissipates these fears, it puts in their place a calm and a certainty that disconcert nature. Look at the martyrs – and not only a St Maurice, the leader of the Theban Legion, accustomed to the struggles of the field of battle, but Felicity, mother of seven children, or Perpetua, noble lady of Carthage for whom the world had only favours, or Agnes, a child of sixteen years, and so many thousands more – and say that the gift of fortitude does not produce sacrifices. What has the fear of death become, that death the mere thought of which can anguish us? And those generous offerings of an entire life immolated in renunciation and privation, in order to find Jesus without division and to follow more closely in his footsteps! And the many lives veiled from the superficial and distracted gaze of other people. Lives whose very element is sacrifice. In which serenity is never overcome by trial. In which the cross that always returns is always accepted! What trophies for the spirit of fortitude! What devotion to duty he knows how to arouse! If human beings on their own are of small consequence, how great they become under the action of the Holy Spirit!

Again, it is the spirit of fortitude which helps Christians brave the sad temptation of human respect, raising them above worldly considerations that would dictate another sort of behaviour. It is the spirit which urges people to prefer the joy of not having violated the Commandment of their God to the vain honour of the world. It is this spirit of fortitude which helps them accept the reverses of fortune as so many merciful designs of heaven, which sustains the courage of Christians in the deeply grievous loss of people dear to them. And in the physical sufferings which would render life a burden, if they did not know that they were visitations by the Lord. It is the spirit of fortitude, finally, as we read in the *Lives* of the Saints, which uses the very repugnances of nature in order to provoke those heroic acts in which the human creature seems to have overcome the limits of it, being in order to elevate itself to the level of the impassable and glorified spirits.

Spirit of fortitude, be ever more present in us and save us from the weakness of this present age. In no other era has the energy of the soul been more weakened, the worldly spirit more triumphant, sensualism more insolent, pride and independence more pronounced. To know how to be firm with oneself is a rarity that excites astonishment in those who witness it: so much have the maxims of the Gospel lost ground! Steady us on this slope that would drag us down as so many others have been dragged down, O divine Spirit! Allow us to address to you in the form of a petition the vows that Paul formulated for the Christians of Ephesus, and permit us to dare to ask of your generosity "that whole armour of God, so that we may be able to withstand on that evil day, and having done everything, to stand firm. Fasten the belt of truth around our waists, and put on the breastplate of righteousness, as shoes for our feet put on whatever will make us ready to proclaim the gospel of peace. Arm us with the shield of faith, with which all the flaming arrows of the evil one will be quenched. Place the helmet of salvation on our heads, and in our hands the sword of the Spirit, which is the word of God" (cf Eph 6:11–17). With the help of this armour, like the Lord in the desert, we will be able to defeat all our adversities. Spirit of fortitude, make it that it be so!

5.
The Gift of Counsel

The gift of fortitude whose necessity we have recognised in the work of the sanctification of the Christian, would not of itself be sufficient to guarantee that this great work reach its conclusion. The Divine Spirit, therefore, has taken care to unite it to another gift that follows from it and warns us of all dangers. This new favour consists in the gift of counsel. The gift of fortitude cannot be left on its own: it needs something to direct it. The gift of knowledge cannot fulfil this role, because although it illuminates the soul regarding its end and regarding the general rules of conduct that it must follow, the gift of knowledge does not give sufficient light regarding the application of the law of God in particular circumstances and regarding the way in which we should govern our lives. In the different situations in which we can find ourselves, in the resolutions that we can be forced to take, we must be able to hear the voice of the Spirit, and it is through the gift of counsel that this divine voice reaches us. It is this voice which tells us, if we wish to hear it, what we must do and what we must avoid, what we must say and what we must not say, what we must keep and what we must renounce. Through the gift of counsel the Holy Spirit acts upon our understanding, at the same time that it acts upon our will with the gift of fortitude.

This precious gift applies to the whole of life. We are in fact continually constrained to determine ourselves, to decide what kind of people we are going to be, by one choice or another. Therefore, the knowledge that the Holy Spirit will never abandon us to ourselves, as long as we are disposed to follow the direction that he imparts to us, is a reason for profound gratitude towards him. How many traps he can help us to avoid! How many illusions he can destroy in us! How many realities he reveals to us! But in order to not lose his inspiration, we must guard ourselves from the natural impulse that perhaps too often determines us, from the rashness that carries us on the wave of passion, from the excessive haste that urges us to judge and act when we have still only seen one side of the matter, and finally from the negligence that induces us to make our decisions at random in the fear that we will wear ourselves out in the search for that which would be the better thing.

The Holy Spirit, with the gift of counsel, liberates us from all these drawbacks and obstacles. He transforms nature, too often excessive when it is not apathetic. He keeps the soul attentive to what is true, to what is good, to what is truly advantageous. He insinuates into the soul that virtue which is the complement of all the others and a 'seasoning' for them. By this we mean to say the virtue of discretion, whose secret the Spirit understands. By means of this virtue the other virtues keep themselves fresh and in harmony, and do not degenerate into defects. Under the direction of the spirit of counsel, the Christian has nothing to fear: the Holy Spirit takes the responsibility for everything upon himself. What does it matter then, if the world blames or criticises, if it is astonished or scandalised! The world believes itself wise; but it does not have the gift of counsel. From this derives the fact that often the resolutions taken under the inspiration of this gift result in goals totally different to those which the world had proposed. It is inevitable that it should be so, because it is to the world that the Lord has said: "For my thoughts are not your thoughts, nor are your ways my ways" (Is 55:8).

With all the ardour of our desires, therefore, let us call for the divine gift that will preserve us from the danger of governing ourselves; but we understand that this gift only dwells in those who esteem it sufficiently to renounce themselves in its presence. If the Holy Spirit finds us detached from human ideas, convinced of our fragility, he will condescend to be our counsel. If, on the contrary, we were to be wise in our own eyes, he would retract his light and abandon us to ourselves.

We do not wish for this to happen to us, Divine Spirit! We know only too well by our own experience that it is of no advantage to us to run the risks of human prudence, and we sincerely renounce before you the pretensions of our spirit so ready to let itself be dazzled and deluded. Conserve in us, and deign to develop in all liberty, this ineffable gift which you have given us in baptism. Be our counsel for ever. "Make us know your ways and teach us your paths. Direct us in the truth and instruct us, because it is from you that salvation comes and this is why we attach ourselves to your conduct" (cf Ps 119). We know that we will be judged on all our works and all our projects, but we also know that we have nothing to fear as long as we are faithful to your guidance. We will therefore be attentive to "listen to what the Lord God says" (cf Ps 85:8), the spirit of counsel, whether he speaks to us directly or whether he refers us to the instrument that he has chosen for us. Blessed be Jesus, therefore, who has sent us his Spirit so that it might be our guide, and blessed be this divine Spirit who deigns always to assist us and whom our past resistance has not distanced from us!

6.
The Gift of Understanding

This sixth gift of the Holy Spirit makes the soul enter onto a way that is superior to the one along which it had been proceeding until now. The first five gifts all tend to actions. The fear of God puts the person back into their just place by giving them humility, piety opens their heart to divine affections. Knowledge makes them discern the way of salvation from the way of perdition. Fortitude arms them for the battle. Counsel directs them in their thoughts and in their works. They can now therefore act and follow their path with the hope of reaching the goal. But the goodness of the divine Spirit has yet other favours in store for them. The Spirit has decided to give them a foretaste in this world of the happiness that is in store for them in the other life. This gift is the means to make their path more secure, to animate their courage and to recompense their efforts. The path of contemplation will therefore be open to them from now on, and the divine Spirit will place them there by means of understanding.

At this word 'contemplation', many people will perhaps become disturbed, wrongly persuaded that it can only be found in the rare conditions of a life lived in retirement and far from the dealings of people. This is a serious and dangerous mistake, a mistake that too often retards the ascent of souls. Contemplation is the state to which every soul that searches for God, in a certain measure, is called. It does not consist in phenomena that it pleases the Spirit to manifest in certain privileged persons, and that he destines to prove the reality of the supernatural life. Contemplation is simply that more intimate relationship which is established between God and the soul that has been faithful to him in its actions. For that soul, provided that it places no obstacle, are reserved two favours, the first of which is the gift of understanding that consists in the illumination of the spirit enlightened henceforth by a higher light.

This light does not take away faith, but illuminates the eye of the soul, fortifying it and giving it a more wide-ranging view of divine things. Many clouds that came from the weakness and coarseness of the soul which had not yet been initiated, are dissipated. The charm-filled beauty of the mysteries, beauty which before had only been felt vaguely, is revealed. Ineffable harmonies which were never guessed, appear. This is not the face-to-face vision which is reserved for the eternal day, but neither is it the weak light which before had directed its steps. The eye of the spirit is shown ways to understand and make sense of what is believed. It is also shown reasons why belief is in fact so 'suitable'. The perception of these things brings a certainty full of sweetness. The soul expands at these illuminations which enrich faith, which make hope grow and love develop. All seems new to the soul and when it looks back, it compares things and sees clearly that the truth, being always the same, is now grasped in an incomparably more complete way.

The narrative of the Gospels impresses it more. In the words of the Saviour it finds a taste unknown to it until now. It understands better the aim that he intended in the institution of his sacraments. The Holy Liturgy moves it with its august formulas and its profound rites. The reading of the *Lives* of the Saints attracts it, nothing astonishes it in their sentiments and actions. It savours the writings of the saints more than any others, and it feels its spiritual well-being enhanced through its contact with these friends of God. Surrounded by duties of every nature, the divine flame guides the soul in order to satisfy each one of them. The very diverse virtues that it must practise are reconciled in its conduct. One is never sacrificed to the other, because the soul sees the harmony that must reign between them. It is far from scrupulosity as it is far from laxity, and always attentive to immediately recoup the losses that it might have incurred. Sometimes, the Spirit even instructs it through an interior word that the soul hears and that illuminates its situation with new light.

From now on the world and its vain errors are appreciated for that which they are, and the soul purifies itself from the attachment and pleasure that it still might have for them. That which had greatness and beauty only according to nature, appears poor and miserable to this eye that the Holy Spirit has opened to the divine and eternal greatnesses and beauties. In the soul's eyes there is one single aspect of this exterior world – this world that deludes carnal beings – which redeems it: the fact that the visible creation, which bears signs of the beauty of God, is capable of serving for the glory of its author. The soul learns to make use of this visible creation with acts of thanksgiving, rendering it supernatural, glorifying with the King-

Prophet him who has left the marks of his beauty on this multitude of beings (who so often cause the loss of the person, while they are called to become steps that should lead the person to God).

The gift of understanding diffuses also in the soul the knowledge of its own way. It helps it to understand how wise and merciful the heavenly designs have been, which have sometimes broken it and taken it to places where it did not think to go. The soul sees that if it had been its own master to dispose of its life as it wished, it would have missed its goal, and that God has made it reach this goal by initially hiding from it the designs of his fatherly wisdom. Now it is happy because it enjoys peace, and its heart does not know how to thank God who has brought it to its destination without consulting it. If it should happen that it be called upon to give its counsels, to exercise spiritual direction out of duty or out of charity, one can trust it. The gift of understanding illuminates it for the sake of others as much as for itself. However, it does not interfere and does not impose its own lessons on those who did not ask for them. But if it is asked it responds and its answers are luminous like the flame which illuminates it.

Such is the gift of understanding, true illumination of the Christian soul, and it makes itself felt to the Christian soul in proportion to the soul's faithfulness in using the other gifts. This is a gift that is conserved by humility, moderation of desires and interior recollection. A dissipated conduct would halt its development and could even stifle it. In a life occupied and filled with duties, in the very midst of inevitable distractions to which the soul lends itself without abandoning itself, this faithful soul can keep itself recollected. If it be therefore simple, if it be small in its own eyes, then that which God hides from the proud and reveals to the lowly (Lk 10:21) will be revealed to it and dwell in it.

No one can doubt that such a gift be an immense help for the salvation and sanctification of the soul. We must therefore implore it from the divine Spirit with all the ardour of our desires, remaining convinced that we will reach it more securely with the fervour of our hearts than with the effort of our spirit. It is true that it is in the understanding that the divine light which is the object of this gift is diffused. But its effusion comes above all from the will warmed by the fire of charity, according to the word of Isaiah, "Believe and you will have understanding" (Is 6:9, thus quoted by the Greek and Latin Fathers according to the Septuagint). Let us turn to the Holy Spirit and using the words of David, let us say to him, "Open our eyes that we might see the marvels of your precepts; give us understanding and we will have life" (cf Ps 119). Instructed by the Apostle, let us present our request in a yet more insistent manner, making our own the prayer that he addresses to the heavenly Father in the name of the faithful of Ephesus, imploring on their behalf: a spirit of wisdom and revelation by which God is known, the eyes of the heart which make known what is the hope to which he has called us, and the riches of the glorious inheritance which God has prepared among the saints (cf Eph 1:17-18).

7.
The Gift of Wisdom

The second favour that the divine Spirit has destined for the soul that is faithful to him in its actions is the gift of wisdom, which is yet greater than that of understanding. This second favour is, however, linked to the first, in the sense that the object which is shown in understanding is tasted and possessed in the gift of wisdom. The Psalmist, inviting people to draw closer to God, recommends the taste of the supreme good, "Taste and see that the Lord is good" (Ps 34:8). Holy Church on the very day of Pentecost asks God for us the favour of tasting the good, *recta sapere,* because the union of the soul with God is more an *experiencing by taste* than it is a *seeing by vision* which would be incompatible with our present state. The light given by the gift of understanding is not direct, it makes the soul rejoice and guides the soul's own understanding towards the truth. But this light finds its fulfilment through the gift of wisdom which is like its end.

Understanding therefore is illumination, and wisdom is union. Now, the union with the highest good comes through the will, that is, through the love which is in the will. We observe this progression in the angelic hierarchies. The Cherub shines with understanding, but yet above him there is the Seraph who is ablaze with love. Love is ardent in the Cherub, just as understanding with its vivid light illuminates the Seraph. But the former is differentiated from the latter by its predominant quality (understanding). And the higher one is the one which attains most intimately to divinity by love, the one which tastes the highest good.

The seventh gift is adorned by the beautiful name of wisdom, and this name comes to it from eternal wisdom to which it tends to assimilate itself through the ardour of its affection. This uncreated wisdom, which condescends to allow itself to be tasted by human beings in this valley of tears, is the divine Word, the very word which the Apostle calls "the splendour of the glory of the Father and the form of his substance" (Heb 1:3). It is the divine Word that has sent us the Spirit to sanctify us and to bring us back to him, so that the most exalted operation of this divine Spirit is to bring about our union with him who, being God, made himself flesh and became obedient unto death, even death on the cross (Phil 2:8). Through the mysteries accomplished in his humanity, Jesus has helped us penetrate even to his divinity. Through the faith illuminated by supernatural understanding, "we have seen glory, glory that he had as the only begotten of the Father, full of grace and truth" (Jn 1:14). And just as he has made himself a participant in our humble human nature, he, who is himself uncreated wisdom, gives himself even in this world to be tasted in the form of this created wisdom. Wisdom which the Holy Spirit forms in us as the most sublime of his gifts.

Happy, therefore, are those in whom this precious wisdom reigns, the wisdom which reveals to the soul the taste of God and of all that belongs to God! The Apostle tells us, "Those who are unspiritual are deprived of this taste, which discerns that which comes from the Spirit of God" (1 Cor 2:14). In order to enjoy this gift they must become spiritual, give themselves with docility to the desire of the Spirit. So it will come to pass in them as in others who, after having been slaves as they were of the carnal life, have been liberated through docility to the divine

Spirit who searched for them and found them. The person who is less coarse, but given to the spirit of the world, is equally impotent to understand what constitutes the object of the gift of wisdom and that which is revealed by the gift of understanding. Such a person judges those who have received this gift and blames them; happy are they if they do not go any further and oppose or persecute them! Jesus says it expressly, "The world cannot receive the Spirit of Truth because it does not see it and does not know it" (Jn 14:17). Let those who have the good fortune to desire the supreme good know that they must be entirely detached from the profane spirit which is the personal enemy of the Spirit of God. Liberated from its chains, they will be able to ascend up to wisdom.

The essence of this gift is that it gives great vigour to the soul and strengthens its powers. The whole of life becomes vigorous, as happens to those who use food which agrees with them. There is no longer any contradiction between God and the soul, and for this reason union is rendered easy. "Where the Spirit of the Lord is, there is freedom", says the Apostle (2 Cor 3:17). All becomes easy for the soul under the action of the Spirit of wisdom. Things which are hard for nature, far from causing surprise, appear sweet, and the heart is no longer frightened by suffering. Not only can one say that God is not far from a soul to which the Holy Spirit has given a disposition such as this, but also that the soul is visibly united to him. Let it keep watch, however, on humility, because pride can still reach up to it, and its fall would be all the more profound for its elevation being greater.

Let us persist with the Holy Spirit and beg him not to refuse us this precious wisdom which will bring us to Jesus, the infinite wisdom. A wise man of the ancient law already aspired to this favour, when he wrote these words of which only the Christian has perfect understanding: "I prayed, and understanding was given me; I called on God, and the spirit of wisdom came to me" (Wis 7:7). We must therefore ask for this gift with insistence. In the New Testament, St James the Apostle invites us to do the same through his even more insistent exhortations: "If any of you is lacking in wisdom, ask God, who gives to all generously and ungrudgingly, and it will be given you" (Jas 1:5). We dare to make this invitation of the Apostle our own, divine Spirit, and we say to you: O you who proceed from the power and the wisdom, give us wisdom. He who is wisdom has sent you to us in order to reunite us to him. Take us beyond ourselves, unite us to him who united himself to our weak nature.

Holy instrument of unity, be the link which will unite us for ever to Jesus, and the one who is the power, and the Father will adopt us "as heirs and joint-heirs with his Son" (Rom 8:17).